Basic
Library
Skills

Basic Library Skills

Fourth Edition

by
Carolyn Wolf

McFarland & Company, Inc., Publishers
Jefferson, North Carolina, and London

British Library Cataloguing-in-Publication data are available

Library of Congress Cataloguing-in-Publication Data

Wolf, Carolyn E., 1941–
    Basic library skills / by Carolyn Wolf. — 4th ed.
      p.   cm.
    Includes bibliographical references and index.
    ISBN 0-7864-0669-0 (sewn softcover : 50# alkaline paper) ∞
    1. Library research — United States.   I. Title.
Z710.W64   1999
025.5'6 — dc21   99-18567
                                       CIP

Manufactured in the United States of America

McFarland & Company, Inc., Publishers
  Box 611, Jefferson, North Carolina 28640

Preface and Acknowledgments

This text is designed to be a self-contained short course in the use of the library, not an exhaustive treatment of the subject. The intent is to provide a quick and easy way to learn to do library research. One could use it as an adjunct to a course in library usage or as part of an introductory English composition course. Also, it might serve as a self-paced instructional sequence for all students. Students have used the first three editions of this book as the major text in a college course in library usage. An author used the text in a graduate course in research methods. These courses included at least 15 hours of classroom instruction. The student should master basic library skills in about 30 to 35 hours. This will vary according to the intellectual skills of the student and his or her study technique. Furthermore, the self-paced design of the text allows students to learn the material at individual speeds.

The author has included only material that is considered essential for mastery of basic library skills. One cannot learn to use the library by working through the text only. Mastery demands "hands on" experience and practice in the library. The concepts in the text are generalizable to all libraries. Materials that were deemed to be too specific were omitted.

The author determined which skills were needed by library users. Each chapter lists the performance skills, called *objectives*. These statements tell the student what is to be learned in the chapter. After studying the materials in each chapter the student should be able to perform the objectives. These objectives are practical and have immediate application for the student. The author omitted theoretical or abstract materials that were unrelated to specific tasks.

Learning psychologists have discovered that students learn more efficiently if they are presented with and attend to stated objectives. Therefore, it is recommended that students attend to the objectives before studying each chapter.

The *exercises* give students hands-on experience by applying rules stated in the text to situations that approach real "research problems." Students also will find the *new or unusual terms* found in the text listed at the back of the chapter. They should be able to define these after studying the text. Bibliographies of examples used in the text and other resources are also included after each chapter.

Finally, the library is the essence of the educational institution. It is unfortunate that some students have negative feelings toward the library. These feelings will become more positive as students learn to use the library. That is the goal of this text.

The author would like to thank the H. W. Wilson Company, OCLC Online Computer Library Center, Gale Research and the American Psychological Association for permission to use examples of their publications:

Figure 8.3 Reprinted with permission of the American Psychological Association, publisher of *Psychological Abstracts* and the PsycINFO database (© 1887–1998 by the American Psychological Association).

Figures 2.2, 8.2, 8.4, 8.5, 11.3, 11.4, 12.2, 12.3 WorldCat™ and FirstSearch® screens were taken from OCLC's database. The screens are used with OCLC's permission. WorldCat™ is a trademark and FirstSearch® is a registered trademark of OCLC Online Computer Library Center, Incorporated.

Figure 12.5 *Contemporary Authors, v. 160.* Edited by Scot Peacock. Copyright © 1998 Gale Research. All rights reserved. Reproduced by permission.

Figure 5.2 *Bibliographic Index,* 1996, page 29. Copyright © 1996 by the H. W. Wilson Company. Material reproduced with permission of the publisher.

Figure 12.1 *Biography Index,* August 1997, page 131. Copyright © 1997 by the H. W. Wilson Company. Material reproduced with permission of the publisher.

Figure 6.2 *Book Review Digest,* January 1998, page 21. Copyright © 1998 by the H. W. Wilson Company. Material reproduced with permission of the publisher.

Figure 5.1 *Cumulative Book Index,* May 1991, volume 94, number 5, page 171. Copyright © 1991 by the H. W. Wilson Company. Material reproduced with permission of the publisher.

Figure 12.6 *Current Biography,* November 1997, page 61. Copyright © 1997 by the H. W. Wilson Company. Material reproduced with permission of the publisher.

Figure 10.2 *Essay and General Literature Index,* 1996, page 192. Copyright © 1996 by the H. W. Wilson Company. Material reproduced with permission of the publisher.

Figure 10.3 *Fiction Catalog,* 1996 supplement, page 75. Copyright © 1997 by the H. W. Wilson Company. Material reproduced with permission of the publisher.

Table of Contents

8. Periodicals and Newspapers

9. On-Line Database Searching, CD-ROM Indexes and Reference Sources

Introduction: A Brief Historical Perspective

The earliest books, especially those written on papyrus, were scrolls. Users stored them in earthen jars to protect them from water, insects and fire. Early civilizations, such as the Egyptians, had libraries and librarians to store these scrolls. The library at Alexandria, Egypt, was one of the largest of the ancient libraries and contained more than 700,000 scrolls. Julius Caesar destroyed most of the library in 47 B.C., and the Christians further damaged it in A.D. 391. Ancient books contain references to the library, part of which still stands, and one may find book titles and the names of some librarians on the walls.

Discoverers have found other ancient libraries. The Library of Assurbanipal at Nineveh, dated at 668–626 B.C., contained about 25,000 clay tablets. Archaeologists have recovered many of these tablets, and about 21,000 of them, whole or fragmentary, are in the British Museum. Many other ancient libraries were destroyed by war and invading barbarians.

During the Dark or Middle Ages, the monastic libraries preserved much of the classical literature and knowledge. The monks copied books in the scriptorium, a writing room–library combination. Many books were not only copied but translated from Greek and other languages. Early medieval universities were located near monasteries that had libraries. Students waited long periods of time and paid large sums of money to scribes who copied books for them.

The invention of printing by movable type is generally credited to Johannes Gutenberg of Mainz, Germany, sometime between 1450 and

1455. Scholars believe that Gutenberg printed the first complete book, a Bible, in 1456. The art of printing spread rapidly across Europe and arrived in the New World in 1539. With the spread of the technology of printing came uses other than the reproduction of Bibles, psalters and other religious books. Broadsheets, pamphlets, newssheets and other forms of spreading information and news were developed. American colonists printed the first book in 1639.

During the mid–18th century came the formation of national libraries. The British Museum, a library and museum, was founded in 1733. The nucleus of the library was the personal collections of Sir Robert Cotton, Robert Harley, Earl of Oxford, and Sir Hans Sloan. The holdings were enlarged in 1757 with the addition of the Royal Library, books collected by the kings from Edward IV to George II. The United States Congress founded the Library of Congress in 1800 as a research library. The British burned the library in 1814 during the attack on Washington. The collection was rebuilt around the personal library of Thomas Jefferson, who was also instrumental in convincing other book collectors to send their personal collections to the library.

Copyright offices have been established in national libraries for developing the national libraries and insuring the completeness of its collection (at a somewhat small cost to the government).

The first public library in the United States was founded in 1833 in Petersborough, New Hampshire. The first major public library was established in Boston in 1852 but was not opened until 1854. In the 1900s, Andrew Carnegie began donating money to communities throughout the country for the construction of libraries. These libraries were to be open to the public free of charge. Often Carnegie built libraries in small rural communities that would have been unable to build their libraries without this financial assistance. Many of these libraries are still in use today.

In 1969 the term "media center" came into general use for the school library. Most of today's institutional libraries are truly media centers, offering non-print resources (such as audio and video recordings) besides traditional printed material. By the mid 1970s library networks, such as OCLC, were formed and libraries began to automate (computerize) their catalogs and share their resources. As computer technology improved and costs decreased more libraries joined networks and more library functions were automated. By the late 1990s most libraries were using computerized catalogs and circulation systems and providing access to their catalogs via the Internet. With the high costs and diversity of materials it is necessary to share resources. Such sharing enables libraries to fulfill their mission; to serve as repositories to recorded history and culture, making information readily available for the individual.

Suggested Readings

Cater, John, ed. *Printing and the Mind of Man: A Descriptive Catalogue Illustrating the Impact of Print on the Evolution of Western Civilization During Five Centuries.* New York: Holt, Rinehart and Winston, 1967.

Christ, Karl. *The Handbook of Medieval Library History.* Metuchen, NJ: Scarecrow, 1984.

Clement, Richard W. *The Book in America: With Images from the Library of Congress.* Golden, CO: Fulcrum Publications, 1996.

Diringer, David. *The Book Before Printing: Ancient, Medieval and Oriental.* New York: Dover, 1982 (reprint of 1953 ed.).

Dunkin, Paul Shaner. *Tales of Melvil's Mouser; or Much Ado About Libraries.* New York: R. R. Bowker, 1970.

Goodrum, Charles A. *The Library of Congress.* New York: Praeger, 1974.

_____. *Treasures of the Library of Congress.* New York: H. N. Abrams, 1980.

Hobson, Anthony Robert Alwyn. *Great Libraries.* London: Weidenfeld & Nicholson, 1970.

Jackson, Donald. *The Story of Writing.* New York: Taplinger, 1981.

Jones, Theodore. *Carnegie Libraries Across America: A Public Legacy.* New York: John Wiley, 1977.

Katz, William A. *Dahl's History of the Book.* 3rd rev. ed. Metuchen, NJ: Scarecrow, 1995.

Keep, Austin Baxter. *The Library in Colonial America.* New York: B. Franklin, 1970.

McMurtrie, Douglas C. *The Book: The Story of Printing and Bookmaking.* New York: Covici, Friede, 1937.

Musmann, Klaus. *Technological Innovations in Libraries, 1860–1960: An Anecdotal History.* Westport, CT: Greenwood Press, 1993.

New York Public Library. *Censorship: 500 Years of Conflict.* New York: Oxford University Press, 1984.

Oswald, John Clyde. *Benjamin Franklin, Printer.* Detroit: Gale Research Company, 1974.

Rosenberry, Cecil R. *For the Government and People of This State: A*

History of the New York State Library. Albany: University of the State of New York, 1970.

Winkler, Paul A. *Reader in the History of Books and Printing.* Englewood, CO: Information Handling Services, 1978.

1. A Walking Tour of the Library

Objectives

After studying this chapter the student shall be able to
- locate the various facilities of the library in a quick and efficient manner
- draw a map indicating where these facilities are
- identify relevant staff members and the services each provides
- find the location of each staff member and show this on the map
- list the hours the library is open and when its constituent services are available
- state the policies of the library in terms of borrowing regulations, open and closed stacks, overdue fines, and the general regulations regarding the use of the building

General Information

The aim of this chapter is to help the student identify and locate basic services offered by the library. To use the library extensively, the student should familiarize himself with its layout, facilities, resources and staff. To do this, a walking tour is essential. Many libraries give official tours by staff members. If these are not available, then the student should take his own tour.

As the student walks through the library he or she should note where all services and materials are located. For future reference a map or schematic diagram is helpful. Since each library is unique, the location of these components will vary greatly. The student should therefore diagram the library that they will use. Some libraries provide maps. These may be very specific or somewhat incomplete. In the latter case, additional information may be added.

The next stop on the walking tour is the circulation desk, since it is the "hub" where most of the business of the library is conducted. The main function of the circulation desk is to keep books moving in and out of the library. Students should familiarize themselves with the rules for book circulation (length of loan period, identification required when checking out books) and the policy for fines and lost books.

Libraries usually have a special system for reserve materials, which may include books, journal articles, tapes and other sources that are set aside for use by students in their courses. There may be special restrictions on the use of these materials. If this reserve area is not located near the circulation desk, a point should be made to find it.

A critical area of the library is the reference section. The reference librarian's main function is to provide help in using the reference materials provided by the library. This person can locate sources to be consulted to answer specific questions. The reference desk is usually located near the entrance or the circulation desk.

On the next stop of the walking tour, the student should locate the card/computerized catalog. Nearly everything the library has is listed here. (The use of the catalog is explained in Chapter 2.) The catalog is usually located near the reference desk. Most libraries have given up the card catalog and are using computer terminals (On-line Public Access — OPAC) and some use microfiche cards. If the library has "closed" and removed its card catalog, then find the computer terminals or microfiche copy (COM) of the catalog. A "closed" catalog means that no cards have been added after the "closed" date and the student must consult the OPACs or COM catalog for recent additions to the library's collection.

A brief walk through the bookshelves (stacks) will enable the user to get a general overview of how the books are grouped. Notice should be taken of the numbering system and how it relates to the catalog. Since the use of the catalog is thoroughly explained in Chapter 2 just a brief overview is necessary during the tour. The student could randomly select a book from the catalog to see if it can be located on the shelves. Special sections, such as fiction, new books and rare books, should be located and added to the map.

Most libraries have a separate area or special reading room for periodicals, magazines and journals. There is usually a periodicals desk or

Checking out books at the circulation desk.

office, which may be staffed by a librarian or student assistants to aid in locating or identifying specific items. Most libraries do not permit the free circulation of periodicals since they have heavy use for short periods of time. The rules for the use of the periodical sections should be studied as they vary between libraries. Some libraries keep back files of newspapers or microfilms of them. The student should locate where these are kept and find out how to use the microfilm readers. Overcrowded libraries may use compact shelves for periodicals. Usually a library staff member will operate these stacks.

A recently burgeoning part of library services is "nonprint" (or non-book") materials. The materials include microprint formats (microfilm, microfiche), audio and video tapes, records, slides, videodiscs, CD's and 16mm and 35mm films. Unfortunately, these materials may be underused because students think they are difficult to use. Students should familiarize themselves with all the materials that are available and with how to operate the equipment. A valuable use of time might be just

Compact shelving saves space, but its operation may require the assistance of a library staff member.

looking at an example from these specific materials and operating the equipment. The location of the materials and the equipment should be noted on the library map.

An important adjunct of the library is the copying service. One should find where services are, how to use them with the various types of materials, and any charges connected with their use. If the machines are coin operated, change should be brought to the library, as some librarians find it distracting and time-consuming to make change! Some libraries do have machines that make change. Some libraries have machines which dispense prepaid cards for use with the copy machines. There may be special copying areas in the library. These should be located and indicated on the map. The prudent use of copying is suggested, and copyright laws should be followed. The student should not make multiple copies of copyrighted materials without permission of the publisher since it is illegal to do so.

The location of certain items that may not appear essential can make the use of the library a more pleasant and efficient experience. Such items include stairs and elevators, lavatories, water fountains, pencil sharpeners, paper cutters and telephones. These should be shown on the map. The student should also include the location of listening rooms for records, CDs and tapes and special areas for typewriters, computers and calculators.

The student should become familiar with the staff of the library. They are there for the user's benefit and are usually eager to help. It is important to remember that the library aides are employed to help find information and expect to be called upon. To the librarian there is no such thing as a "stupid question."

Libraries generally divide their staff into two major departments, public services and technical services. The public services employees are "up front" and interact with the library patrons or visitors. They work at the circulation, reference, reserve and periodical desks. Knowing the names of the people who work in the public services areas may be useful. The technical services employees are the "behind-the-scenes" staff. They are usually divided into two departments, cataloging and acquisitions. The acquisitions staff is responsible for purchasing books, periodicals, nonprint and other materials and may be consulted if students wish the library to purchase materials on an individual basis. The cataloging staff is responsible for adding new acquisitions to the catalog and making resources ready for the shelves and circulation. Finally, the head librarian supervises all staff and is available to solve problems that

Taking time to browse in the stacks.

cannot be handled by the staff. The name and location of the head librarian's office should be noted.

The rules, regulations and policies of the library are instituted and maintained for the benefit of the users. A copy of the library manual should be obtained and some of these questions should be answered by referring to the manual: What services are available at what hours? What are the borrowing regulations? What are the rules for the reserve materials? What are the fines for overdue books? What is the policy on lost books? Does the library permit smoking, eating or drinking and where are these things permitted? What are the security precautions? (Knowing these may avoid embarrassment when leaving the library.)

After the tour the student should complete a map containing the following locations:

1. circulation desk
2. reference desk
3. reserve desk
4. reference section
5. periodicals section
6. reading room
7. book stacks
8. newspapers
9. microfilm section
10. readers
11. copying machines
12. head librarian's office
13. cataloging department
14. acquisitions department
15. card catalog (or OPAC)
16. special collections
17. rare book room
18. lavatories
19. water fountains
20. pencil sharpener(s)
21. stairs and elevators
22. exits
23. smoking areas
24. computers for public use
25. computer software
26. atlases
27. public telephones

A list of people who work in the library should contain at least the names of the following:

1. head librarian
2. circulation department head
3. reference department head
4. periodicals department head
5. cataloging department head
6. acquisitions department head

Exercises for Chapter 1

1. Complete a map locating the facilities listed earlier.
2. List the name(s) of the person(s) responsible for various library services.
3. Complete the following chart of library hours:

	Library Opens	Library Closes
Sunday		
Monday		
Tuesday		
Wednesday		
Thursday		
Friday		
Saturday		

4. (A) For what period of time may an open shelf book be charged out?
   (B) A reserve book?
5. (A) What is the *daily* fine for an overdue book?
   (B) What is the *hourly* fine for an overdue book?
6. Does the library have closed stacks? If so, how do you get books?

Important Terms in Chapter 1

circulation	*periodicals*
"closed catalog"	*public services*
reserve	*technical services*
reference	*stacks*

2. The Catalog and Cataloging Systems

Objectives

After studying this chapter the student shall be able to
- distinguish among microfiche, card and computer catalogs
- use call numbers to locate materials anywhere in the library
- use either the Dewey Decimal system or the Library of Congress system to locate materials
- use alphabetical filing rules to locate catalog units
- interpret all the information found in catalog entries

The Catalog

Catalogs contain all the books owned by a particular library. Trying to use the library without referring to the catalog is like looking for the proverbial needle in a haystack. Besides showing what a library owns, the catalog supplies information about each holding. Most libraries catalog their pamphlets, records, tapes, microforms and other resources as well as books. A card catalog is a series of cabinets filled with 3 × 5 cards in drawers.

Most libraries are no longer using a card catalog. Some have the same information on microfiche, magnetic tape or CDs. Most libraries use a computerized catalog, often referred to as an OPAC or Online Public Access Catalog. Microfiche catalogs are frequently called COM (computer output microfiche) and are computer-produced. They are updated frequently. Colleges and universities that use COM will probably have COM readers available in many places on the campus outside the library, such as classrooms, dorms and faculty offices. Other libraries have their catalog on magnetic tape or CD, which require the use of a computer terminal. Libraries locate terminals throughout the library and sometimes in locations outside the library. Libraries that have an on-line catalog (OPAC — On-line Public Access Catalog) may also allow access from remote computers via the internet. Additional information about OPACs will be found in Chapter 3. Libraries with their holdings on computer tapes (database) sometimes print out copies of part of the catalog and have these available for general campus use. These print-outs are updated on a regular basis.

The library lists most items in the catalog by subject, by author and by title. Fiction and autobiography, however, usually do not have subject entries. There are two ways to organize the card catalog. The "dictionary catalog" organizes all the units (cards) in one alphabetical file. The "divided catalog" is organized in two alphabetical sequences, one for subject units and one for author and title units. These two sequences are clearly labeled, and consultation in both segments may be necessary to determine all listings.

The Catalog Contents

When you consult the catalog you will find the following types of information. If you are using a card catalog (a cabinet with drawers, filled with cards) the author card is generally the main entry. See Figure 2.1A for an example of an author card. Figure 2.1B also includes the author entry (for the same book) from an OPAC. All author cards or entries provide information in the following order (* if applicable).

1. author's name
2. birth and death dates *
3. title
4. subtitle*
5. coauthor's name*
6. notes on editor, compiler, illustrator*
7. edition number*
8. place of publication

Figure 2.1

AUTHOR   Wolf, Carolyn E., 1941-
TITLE   Indians of North and South America : a bibliography : based on
              the collection at the Willard E. Yager Library-Museum, Hartwick
              College, Oneonta, N.Y. / compiled by Carolyn E. Wolf and Karen
              R. Folk.
IMPRINT   Metuchen, N.J. : Scarecrow Press, 1977.
DESCRIPT   ix, 576 p. ; 23 cm.
NOTE   Includes indexes.
SUBJECT   Indians -- Bibliography -- Catalogs.
SUBJECT   Indians -- Bibliography -- Catalogs.   **A**
              Willard E. Yager Library-Museum.
ADD AUTHOR Folk, Karen R.
              Willard E. Yager Library-Museum.

LOCATION	CALL NO.	STATUS
Perm. Res.	Z1209 .W82	AVAILABLE
Yager Coll.	Z1209 .W82 c.2	AVAILABLE
Yager Coll.	Z1209 .W82 c.3	AVAILABLE
Reference	Z1209 .W82 c.4	AVAILABLE

Ref.
Z
1209
W82

Wolf, Carolyn E., 1941-   , comp.
    Indians of North and South America :
a bibliography : based on the
collection at the Willard E. Yager
Library-Museum, Hartwick College,
Oneonta, N.Y. / compiled by Carolyn E.
Wolf and Karen R. Folk. Metuchen, N.J.
: Scarecrow Press, 1977.

B   ix, 576 p. ; 23 cm.
    Includes indexes.

    1. Indians--Bibliography--Catalogs.
2. Willard E. Yager Library-Museum.
I. Folk, Karen R., joint author.
II. Willard E. Yager Library-Museum.
III. Hartwick College authors. Faculty.
IV. Title

NONEOH 158340   VZHMdc   77-1759

   9. publishing company
  10. date of publication or copyright
  11. subject headings*
  12. other added entries*

The author's name is on the top line. Carolyn E. Wolf is the author of
the book in Figure 2.1. The next line is indented and contains the title

of the book, *Indians of North and South America*. The subtitle is *a bibliography: based on the collection at the Willard E. Yager Library-Museum, Hartwick College, Oneonta, N.Y.* The next piece of information concerns the two compilers, Carolyn E. Wolf and Karen R. Folk. The book was published in Metuchen, N.J., by Scarecrow Press in 1977.

The number to the left of the author's name is the call number. This number allows retrieval of the item.

Unfortunately most students do not pay attention to the rest of the information on the card or in the entry. Some information can be very useful in selecting books before going to the shelves. The line of information after the publication data contains the collation, which is information about the number of pages in the book (576) and the height of the book (23 cm). At first glance the height of a book might seem irrelevant, but this may be a vital clue to locating a book. Some libraries store oversized books on special shelves.

The card in Figure 2.1B also has a note, this book includes indexes. Sometimes a note may include a summary of the book's contents. Information in these notes can be particularly useful if the student needs a book that specifically includes a bibliography, illustrations, maps or other resources. The numbered items near the bottom of the card are referred to as added entries. They include all the subject headings assigned to this book (those with Arabic numbers) plus other cards/entries in the catalog for the title, co-author or series (those with Roman numerals). This book by Wolf has two subject headings assigned to it and is therefore accessible by searching either subject heading. There is also an entry for the title, co-author and for the museum. Figure 2.1A also includes an OPAC entry for the same title. The information is in the same order as on the catalog card. This particular library puts the call number at the bottom of the entry. You will note that this library had four copies of this title. The LOCATION tag indicates that copies can be found in three different locations: Permanent Reserve, Reference, and in the Yager Collection (a special collection).

Figure 2.2 is the author entry for the second edition of this work. The collation notes also include the ISBN — international standard book number for that edition. Figure 2.2 contains both the author card from a card catalog (A) and the author entry from an OPAC (B, C). Note that the OPAC entry includes tags at the left of each line in the entry. The tag describes the information on that line, such as AUTHOR, TITLE, EDITION, IMPRINT, DESCRIPT (collation), BIBLIOG, SUBJECT, and ADDED AUTHOR. The number of tags will vary depending on the

Figure 2.2

```
Z
718.7       Wolf, Carolyn E., 1941-
.W64            Basic library skills / Carolyn Wolf,
1986        Richard Wolf. -- 2nd ed. -- Jefferson,
            N.C. : McFarland, c1986.
                xi, 141 p., [1] leaf of plates : ill. ; 23 cm.
            Includes bibliographies and index.
            ISBN 0-89950-223-8 (pbk.)
```

A

```
            1. Libraries and students.  2. Study,
        Method of.  I. Wolf, Richard, 1938-
        II. Title          III. Hartwick College authors.
        Faculty.
```

NONEOH 20 JAN 87   13333492   VZHMdc   85-43600

AUTHOR   Wolf, Carolyn E., 1941-
TITLE   Basic library skills / Carolyn Wolf, Richard Wolf.
EDITION   2nd ed.
IMPRINT   Jefferson, N.C. : McFarland, c1986.
DESCRIPT   xi, 141 p., [1] leaf of plates : ill. ; 23 cm.   **B**
BIBLIOG.   Includes bibliographies and index.
SUBJECT   Libraries and students.
           Study skills.
ADD AUTHOR Wolf, Richard, 1938-

AUTHOR   : Wolf, Carolyn E., 1941-
TITLE   : Basic library skills / Carolyn Wolf, Richard Wolf
EDITION   : 2nd ed
PUBLISHER   : Jefferson, N.C. : McFarland
DATE   : c1986
DESCRIPTION : xi, 141 p., [1] leaf of plates : ill. ; 23 cm.
DOCUMENT TYPE : Reference.
SUBJECTS   : Libraries and students.
            Study skills.   **C**

2 item(s):
SUNY Oneonta - Reference Collection, 1st floor
    REF Z718.7 .W64 1986   For use in library only

SUNY Oneonta - Special Collections (Ask at Reference Desk)
    SCC Z718.7 .W64 1986   For use in library only

Figure 2.2 (cont.)

AUTHOR   Wolf, Carolyn E., 1941-
TITLE   Basic library skills
EDITION   3rd ed.
IMPRINT   Jefferson, N.C. : McFarland, 1993
DESC.   xiii, 177 p. : ill. ; 23 cm.
NOTE   Includes bibliographical references and index.
      PUBLICATION TYPE: Book
SUBJECT   Libraries United States.
      Searching, Bibliographical.
      Libraries
      United States
ADD AUTHOR Wolf, Richard, 1938-
OCLC CODES LIBRARIES: STATE: NY LIBRARY: AVD BUF CFN CFP SDE VHB
      VVR VVX VXU VYG VZE VZN VZV XQM YCM YJJ YJL YJM YON YSM
      YYP ZQP ZSJ ZUD ZVM ZVT ZXC

D

P > PRINT   R > RETURN to browse   A > ANOTHER TITLE Search
F > FORWARD   T > Show MARC TAG   N > NEW search
B > BACKWARD   S > items with same SUBJECT   E > Mark item for EXPORT
Choose one (P,F,B,R,T,S,A,N,E)

contents of the book or document. Individual libraries may use different tags. Note the differences in the tags for each library. Note the differences in how the call number is displayed for Hartwick College (B) and SUNY Oneonta (C). The last entry is from WorldCat (D) searched through Hartwick College's III (Innovative Interfaces Inc, INNOPAC) Z39.50 option. Note that the WorldCat (D) and Hartwick College (B) displays are nearly identical. However the WorldCat entry also displays the OCLC symbols for all libraries in New York State that also own a copy of this title. Z39.50 is a computer protocol which allows users at Library A to search the catalog of Library B using the same search commands or menus that are used by Library A. Not all libraries have Z39.50 available on the catalogs.

In the early 1980s the Library of Congress stopped printing cards. Some book publishers, jobbers and dealers print cards and supply them with the books. Libraries that are members of OCLC (see Chapter 14) have their cards printed by computers at OCLC. The catalog cards in Figures 2.1B and 2.2A were printed by OCLC. Some libraries may use other computerized systems to produce similar appearing cards.

The Call Number

Libraries use either the Dewey Decimal Classification System or the Library of Congress Classification System. The call number, in the upper left hand corner of the card, or on the bottom of the computer screen shows which system is being used. A Library of Congress call number begins with one, two or three *letters* whereas the call number in the Dewey Decimal system starts with a *number*. Melvil Dewey devised the decimal system in the 19th century while a student at Amherst College. The Amherst Library was in disorder (as were most large libraries of the time) and it was impossible to find specific books. Dewey used a numerical system to arrange the books and submitted it to the Amherst Library Committee for consideration. Many libraries throughout the world still use his system.

Understanding of the Dewey system helps to find books by browsing and is also helpful in selecting books using the catalog. Dewey divided all knowledge into nine categories, numbering them 100 through 900, and put all the general reference works (dictionaries, encyclopedias, newspapers, etc.) into the category 000. Figure 2.3 shows Dewey's general system headings.

Each of these general categories is broken down into nine specific categories and each of these into nine or more specific categories. Then, by adding a decimal point, the system can be expanded continuously. Figure 2.4 contains an example of the 500 category broken down into subcategories. For instance, 540 contains Chemistry and Allied Sciences; 590 contains Zoological Sciences. Subcategory 590 can be broken down into the types of Zoological Sciences, such as 591 for (general) Zoology and 599 for Mammals. Likewise 599 can be broken down by using decimals, 599.1 *Monotremata* and 599.9 *Hominidae*. Similarly the .9 categories could be broken down into .91, .92 and so on depending on the specificity needed. A manual is available that contains all the categories in the Dewey system.

As useful as the Dewey system is, it is inefficient for large libraries. Around the turn of the century the Library of Congress, which used no real classification system, was chaotic. Users could not access many materials. Many other materials were hopelessly lost. In 1899 Herbert Putnam was appointed librarian of Congress and began an effort to get the library's materials in order. A study showed that the Dewey system was ineffectual in dealing with such a large library. The staff and other

Figure 2.3

000 General Works
100 Philosophy and Psychology
200 Religion
300 Social Science
400 Language
500 Pure Science
600 Technology (Applied Science)
700 The Arts
800 Literature
900 History

librarians continued devising a classification system that would be usable with the library's unorganized and rapidly growing collection.

Besides devising the classification system for the Library of Congress, Putnam felt that it was not really necessary for every library to read and catalog the same books. He thought it would be preferable for the Library of Congress to do that work and then share its work with other libraries. He also offered to sell copies of the cards printed by the Library of Congress for its own collection. Librarians eagerly received his ideas since cataloging and card production are time-consuming tasks. Libraries worldwide use the cataloging and card copy produced by the Library of Congress.

The Library of Congress system uses one of 21 letters of the alphabet as the first letter of the classification number. A second or third letter may be added to make up the first part of the classification or call number. Using letters provides more categories than the Dewey system. The system leaves some letters unassigned to provide for undiscovered knowledge. Other letters like O are not used because they may be easily confused with the number 0 (zero). The second line of the LC call number is a number from 1 to 9999. Often these two lines make up the subject part of the call number.

Figure 2.5 contains the general categories in the LC system. For example, B contains Philosophy, Psychology and Religion and N contains Fine Arts. Fine Arts, N, can be further subdivided by adding a second letter. For example, in Figure 2.6 NA is Architecture and NE is Engraving. Also further categories can be devised by adding numbers on the next line, as illustrated in Figure 2.7 (this figure shows just the beginning of the NE tables). As is the case in the Dewey system, the LC system has manuals describing all the various categories.

Figure 2.4

500 Pure Science
510 Mathematics
520 Astronomy and Allied Science
530 Physics
540 Chemistry and Allied Science
550 Science of the Earth and the Other Worlds
560 Paleontology — Paleozoology
570 Life Sciences
580 Botanical Sciences
590 Zoological Sciences
    591 Zoology
    592 Invertebrates (animal plankton and neuston)
    593 Protozoa and Other Simple Animals
    594 Mollusca and Molluscoidea
    595 Other Invertebrates
    596 Chordata Vertebrata (craniata, vertebrates)
    597 Cold Blooded Vertebrates — Pisces (fish)
    598 Aves (birds)
    599 Mammalia (mammals)
        599.1 Momotremata
        599.2 Marsupialia
        599.3 Unguiculata
        599.4 Chiroptera (bats)
        599.5 Cetacea and Sirenia
        599.6 Paenungulata
        599.7 Fernungulata and Tubulidentata
        599.8 Primates
        599.9 Hominidae (humankind and forebears)

To review, the first line of the Dewey number and (generally) the first two lines of the LC number refer to the topic of the book. These call numbers then provide a means of keeping all the books on the same topic in the same section of the library. Both systems also include another line of the call number for the particular author found under the subject indicated. The author line starts with the first letter of the author's last name (see Figure 2.1 again: W for Wolf). This letter then may be followed by a number of additional numbers. These numbers provide finer discriminations, that may be necessary in extremely large libraries

Figure 2.5

A General Works	M Music
B Philosophy, Psychology, Religion	N Fine Arts
	P Language
C History — Auxiliary Sciences	Q Science
D History — Except America	R Medicine
E–F America	S Agriculture, Plant and Animal Industry
G Geography, Anthropology, Sports	
	T Technology
H Social Sciences	U Military Sciences
J Political Science	V Naval Sciences
K Law	Z Bibliography, Libraries, Library Science
L Education	

Figure 2.6

N   Fine Arts
NA Architecture
NB Sculpture
NC Graphic Arts, Drawing and Design
ND Painting
NE Engraving
NK Art Applied to Industry, Decoration and Ornament

but will not be further discussed here. Thus the first line of the call number in Dewey and usually the first two lines in LC denote the subject of the book. The next line (often the last line) is the alphabetic listing of authors within that subject. This system makes it convenient to "browse" through the stacks and to find information without using the catalog. The call numbers also can be thought of as the "address" of the book: it tells the user exactly where that specific book can be found in the library.

To locate materials, the call number in the catalog must be matched with the shelf area location. The book's call number must be copied exactly as it appears in the catalog since each item has a unique number. Once the individual becomes familiar with the location of the shelves, a piece of material can be located quickly, since librarians mark the shelves with a label at one or both ends of the stack.

It should be noted that some libraries have an "oversized" book section. Books that are too large for the regular shelves are put in special sections. For example, many art books are oversized and may be found

Figure 2.7

NE ENGRAVING
1 Periodicals
   10 Yearbooks
   20 Encyclopedias
   25 Dictionaries
   30 Directories
      Exhibitions (by Place)
   40 International
   45 Others
      Museums. Collections
      Public (Art Galleries, Print Departments, etc.)
   53 American
   55 European
      Private
   57 United States
   59
      Sales Catalogs
   63 Before 1801
   65 Auction Catalogs 1801–
   70 Dealers' Catalogs 1801–
   75 Publishers' Catalogs 1801–

in this section. If the student is unable to locate materials on the shelves, he or she should **ask the librarian**. The librarian will be able to tell the student if a particular book is on reserve, out in circulation or in some special section. Many libraries will recall books in circulation or put a "hold" (held/reserves upon return for the person requesting) on the book; when the book is returned the requesting individual is notified.

Filing Rules—Alphabetizing

An understanding of some of the rules for filing cards in the catalog may facilitate the use of the catalog. Catalogers or computers file cards word by word rather than letter by letter. Thus **New York** comes before **news**. Personal names beginning with **Mac** and **Mc** are interfiled (filed together) as if they were all spelled **Mac**. Words which begin with **mac** (e.g., machete) will be interfiled with the personal names — see Figure 2.8.

If "A," "An" or "The" is the first word of the title, the filer or computer ignores it. If it appears any place in the title other than the first word, it is considered when filing. If the title is in a foreign language and the title begins with the equivalent of "a," "an" or "the" (for example, Der, Das, La, Le), the word is ignored when filing. Cards are filed by the first (topmost) line on the card. It may be the author's name, the title, the subject or the name of the series.

Figure 2.8

MacArthur	McGregor
McClusky	machete
MacDonald	machine
mace	MacIntosh

Words that are commonly abbreviated are filed as if they were spelled out. For example, **St.** is filed as **Street** or **Saint** (as the case may be), **Dr.** as if written **Doctor**, and **U.S.** as if written **United States**. However, since **Mrs.** is not everywhere equated with "mistress," it is filed as **M-R-S**, whereas **Mr.** is filed as if it were **Mister**.

Words which may be written as one word, two words or hyphenated are interfiled. For example, folksong, folk-song or folk song would all be interfiled, as would text book and text-book. Hyphenated words or names are filed as separate words except when the first word is a prefix: **bull-dog** is filed as two words, **anti-semitism** or **pre-raphaelite** are filed as one.

Numerals and numbers are filed as spoken; thus **1910** is nineteen ten and **VII** is seven.

Initials and acronyms are filed before words beginning with the same letter, and each letter is filed as if it were a word. Thus **FORTRAN** (think of it as F.O.R.T.R.A.N.) comes before **Fables**.

A personal name comes before a subject, e.g., **Wood, Joseph** comes before **WOOD**.

If you are using an OPAC, these filing rules are observed by the computer and are invisible to the user. For example, if you enter the word THE as the first word of a title, the computer will automatically ignore it.

Figure 2.9

AUTHOR   Neusner, Jacob, 1932-
TITLE   The enchantments of Judaism : rites of transformation from birth
     through death / by Jacob Neusner.
IMPRINT   Atlanta, Ga. : Scholars Press, c1991.
DESCRIPT   xv, 224 p. ; 23 cm.
SERIES   South Florida studies in the history of Judaism ; 21.
BIBLIOG.   Includes bibliographical references (p. 217-219) and indexes.
SUBJECT   Judaism -- Customs and practices -- Meditations.
     Jewish way of life -- Meditations.

LOCATION   CALL NO.   STATUS
Main Library   BM700 .N48 1991   AVAILABLE

Exercises for Chapter 2

1. Look up the subject headings TENNIS and GOLF in LCSH. Record all headings, subheadings, notes, etc. that are listed. Record, if any, the BT, RT, NT, etc. headings.
2. Using the catalog find the call numbers of the following books. Record the call numbers and then locate the books on the shelves.
   (A) *McGraw-Hill Encyclopedia of Science and Technology*
   (B) *Oxford English Dictionary*
   (C) *World Almanac and Book of Facts*
   (D) *Guide to the Presidency*
   (E) *Famous First Facts*
3. Using figures 2.3 and 2.4, give the most specific call number you can for the following books:
   (A) *Basic Astronomy*
   (B) *Introduction to Human Anatomy*
   (C) *The Great Apes of Africa*
   (D) *Encyclopedia Americana*
4. Using figures 2.5, 2.6 and 2.7, give the most specific category you can find for the following books:
   (A) *Custer's Last Stand*
   (B) *A History of American Education*
   (C) *Paintings of Pablo Picasso*
   (D) *Early Copper Engravings*

(E) *Pediatric Surgery*
(F) *New York Times Encyclopedia of Sports*
5. The following questions should be answered by consulting the catalog entry reproduced in Figure 2.9.
(A) What is the publication date?
(B) In what city was this book published?
(C) What is the LC call number?
(D) What is the author's name?
(E) What is the series title?
(F) How many subject headings have been assigned to this book?
(G) What is the title of this book?
(H) Does this book have illustrations?
(I) Who published this book?

Important Terms in Chapter 2

microfiche	*catalog*
COM	*subject headings*
cross-reference	*Dewey system*
LC subject headings	*OPAC*

Important Books for Chapter 2

American Library Association. *ALA Filing Rules*. Chicago: American Library Association, 1980.

_____. *ALA Rules for Filing Catalog Cards*, 2nd ed. Prep. by ALA Editorial committee. Subcommittee on the ALA Rules for Filing Catalog Cards. Pauline A. Seely, chairman and editor. Chicago: American Library Association, 1968.

Comaromi, John P., ed., and Margaret J. Warren, asst. ed. *Manual on the Use of the Dewey Decimal Classification*, 19th ed. Albany, NY: Forest Press/Lake Placid Education Foundation, 1980. The 20th edition, 1993, is also available on CD-ROM from OCLC (the 120th year celebration).

Dewey, Melvil. *A Classification and Subject Index, for Cataloging and Arranging the Books and Pamphlets of a Library*. New York: Gordon Press, 1979. (Reprint of the 1876 ed. published in Amherst, MA.)

Jefferson, Thomas. *Thomas Jefferson's Library: A Catalog with the Entries in His Own Hand*. Edited by James Gilreath and Douglas L. Wilson. Washington, Library of Congress: GPO, 1989.

United States. Library of Congress. Subject Cataloging Division. *Classification; Classes A–Z*. Washington, DC: GPO, 1971– .

Warwick, Robert T. *Using OCLC Under Prism*. New York: Neal-Schuman, 1997.

3. On-Line Public Access Catalogs

Objectives

After studying this chapter the student shall be able to
- recognize and use Boolean operators
- identify different search procedures for OPACs and card catalogs
- access OPACs via the Internet

Definitions

On-Line—A computer user's ability to interact with the databases.

OPAC—(On-Line Public Access Catalog) The library's computerized catalog that replaces the card catalog and is available to anyone using the library.

CD-ROM—(Compact Disk—Read Only Memory) An optical disk, single sided, with read only memory. Many contain audio or data impressed at time of manufacture. May contain commercial databases.

Remote Access—Communicating with a database via a communication link (phone line).

Dial-Up—Using a telephone line to "dial" or call another computer.

Keyword—A significant word in a title, subject or author's name.

KWIC—(Keyword in Context) A type of indexing that allows searching by any term in any part of the record.

Boolean Operators—(and, or, not, near, with, except, in) Terms used to narrow or broaden searches.

MaRC—(Machine Readable Cataloging) The cataloging of library resources using standardized rules and symbols which various computer programs can read, then print and reorganize the data as desired.

Bar Code— A series of lines varying in thickness, making up a code that is read by an optical scanner.

Gateway— Means of connecting one computer terminal of a network with another terminal or computer of a different network.

Protocol— A set of formats or conventions that allow computers to communicate over data transmission (phone) lines.

Network— An interconnection of computers or nodes by communication facilities (phone lines).

LAN—(Local Area Network) A means of connecting computers that share programs, data, databases, often used in offices, schools, etc.

Internet— an outgrowth of the ARPAnet (a U.S. Defense Department experimental network) and other networks. Currently it is a cooperative system connecting computer networks worldwide. Every user of every computer on the Internet has an address. Addresses have suffixes, which provide information about the location or type of network. For example

> .com — a company
> .gov — a governmental agency or office
> .edu — an educational site in the U.S.
> .net — a network
> .mil – military
> .ca — Canada
> .Uk — Great Britain

World Wide Web (WWW)— a loosely organized set of computer sites that provide free information that anyone world wide can read via the Internet. Most sites use HTTP (HyperText Transfer Protocol).

Telnet— a program that allows one computer to act as a terminal for a remote computer network via the Internet. Telnet provides a direct path to the remote computer.

Hytelnet— A site that allows access to all library catalogs (OPACs) by using Telnet. All catalogs are organized first by geographical region, then by country, and then by type.

Vendor— a supplier of services, equipment or supplies.

General Information

Many libraries have "closed" their card catalogs and are no longer adding cards. These libraries have a COM catalog (see Chapter 2) or an on-line catalog, usually called an OPAC (On-Line Public Access Catalog). The libraries that have public access catalogs also will have open computer terminals and some form of instruction on how to search the on-line catalog. On-line catalogs can now be found in public libraries, public school libraries (elementary through high school), college and university libraries and special libraries. Many of these on-line catalogs provide more access points in searching than the old card catalog. Libraries that have officially "closed" their card catalog often do not physically remove the cards. This permits a transition period for those people who are learning to use computers. Some libraries *must* keep their old card catalogs, since the old cards are not yet stored in the computer database. Both card catalog and database must be consulted. If there is a power failure or a computer malfunction occurs, the card catalog serves as a backup.

Libraries which have an OPAC have generally automated (computerized) all the library's operations: circulation, cataloging, periodical check-in and binding, reserves and other daily library procedures. All the daily operations then appear in the public catalog. Thus, when searching the catalog the student is informed of the status of the item, such as "on the shelf," "out in circulation," "on reserve," "on order," or "at the bindery." The catalog also shows the latest issue of a periodical that the library has received and on some systems what date the next issue is expected to arrive. Some circulation systems will generate overdue notices to remind patrons that books should be returned.

Most OPACs allow remote access, that is, if you know the address it is possible dial-up the library computer from a computer outside the library. Then one searches the library's catalog as if you were in the library. Some OPACs have a "gateway" or system allowing the user to access other computers or remote periodical indexes. There is sometimes a charge for using this type of "gateway." Some libraries have bulletin boards or newsletters with information about the school or community that can be accessed from the OPAC "gateway."

Libraries using OPACs generally have printed instructions at the terminal and provide on-line help. If the student has difficulty while searching, a help command gives additional onscreen instructions. Some terminals attached to the OPAC will have printers. The individuals

Public catalogs are often located near the reference desk.

borrowing from libraries using OPACs will need a special card that will have a bar code.

Searching the OPAC

OPACs allow searching by author, title, and subject just as with the card catalog, CD-ROM or COM catalog. In each case it is necssary to

Figure 3.1
A main menu for starting a search on an OPAC

Hartwick College
Stevens-German Library
Welcome to the On-line Public Catalog

A   AUTHOR
T   TITLE
B   AUTHOR/TITLE
S   SUBJECT
W WORDS
C   CALL NO

P Repeat PREVIOUS Search
I Library INFORMATION
R   RESERVE Lists
G CONNECT to indexes and other libraries

D DISCONNECT
   Choose one (A,T,B,S,W,C,P,I,R,G,D)

following the directions for that particular system. Some systems use a series of menus from which the user selects the desired type of search. Other systems require the user to type in a command to select the type of desired search. Often a mnemonic system is employed. Because the computer can read all the words in each entry it is possible to provide additional points of access. It is possible to do a keyword search, one on which the computer looks for a word anyplace it appears in the author index, title index or subject index. Some systems allow free text keyword searching, that is the systems search for that word anyplace in the record. Some systems also allow the use of Boolean searching in the keyword search and may provide searching by ISBN, ISSN or OCLC number. Some systems allow searching by call number, a means of browsing the shelves without going to the shelf. This is particularly useful if the library has closed stacks. Some systems allow searches to be revised without starting over, a blessing for those who can't type. Some systems allow the limiting of a search by date, a range of dates, or by language.

When doing an author search, the author's name should be searched last name first, just as in the card catalog. It is generally not necessary to put commas between names. One may enter just the last name or as many letters of the last name as are known (a truncated or shortened term). Some systems require the entry of a special symbol to show a truncated entry, e.g., "?," "*" or "#." For example it is possible to enter **Green?** The system will then display *all* the authors whose last name begins with those letters and the student can then choose the desired entry. For example — Green, Greenblat, Greene, Greenstone, Greentree, etc. When searching by author, it is sometimes possible to enter altnerative spellings using Boolean operators and doing just one search, e.g., Green or Greene. This is preferable to using the truncated search as it eliminates all except the two possible spellings of the name.

Title searches also allow the student to enter as many words as are known and the OPAC will display on the screen *all* the books that start with those words (see Figure 3.2 titles beginning with the word "**beach**" and with the words "**little house**"). The desired title can then be selected from the list. It is sometimes permissible to use truncated words in title searches.

Figure 3.2

Search: T = BEACH
LINE #   ---------------------------TITLE--------------------------
1   Beach and Sea Animals
2   Beach at St. Addressee
3   Beach Ball
4   The Beach Before Breakfast
5   Beach Bird
6   Beach Birds
7   The Beach Book and the Beach Bucket
8   The Beach Boys
(MORE)

Search: T = LITTLE HOUSE
LINE #   ---------------------------TITLE--------------------------
1   The Little House

2   The Little House; a new math story game
3   The Little House Books
4   The Little House Cookbook: Frontier Food from Laura
5   Little House in the Big Woods
6   Little House in the Ozarks
7   A Little House of Your Own
8   Little House on the Prairie
(MORE)

Subject searches may present the most difficulty as some systems require that the subject entered match *exactly* with Library of Congress subject headings. Incorrect subject headings may lead to no matches.

Also, if the student has not consulted LCSH (Library of Congress Subject Headings, see Chapter 4) guessing correct headings is even more difficult. Some systems are "kinder" ("user friendly") than others and instead of saying "no match," provide an alphabetical list of terms that surround the heading entered. Some systems also provide cross references and show the number of entries for each cross reference. This feature allows the student to choose other subjects without rekeying the search.

Some systems allow the student to combine the author's name and the book title in one search. If the author's name is common or the author has published many books (e.g. Shakespeare) this option provides fewer "hits" and is more likely to display the desired title with fewer steps.

Keyword searches often produce the largest number of entries and so it is necessary to devise a good search strategy. See the following section on Boolean searching.

In many ways OPACs are just elaborate card catalogs and we should not expect more than they can provide. Some systems display a message "no match" on your search term; the same result is sometimes obtained when searching a card catalog. Other systems are more helpful, providing cross references and other words that appear before and after the search term entered.

Some card catalogs also provide cross references and by flipping through the cards in a card catalog, we, of course, find the words before and after the term searched. Librarians say that many students spend more time using the OPAC than a card catalog. An OPAC is constantly developing and changing.

Boolean Searching

In those OPACs that include Boolean search capabilities the Boolean operators generally include "and," "or," and "not." Boolean searches can be done in other types of databases such as periodical indexes on CD-ROM or via on-line vendos such as DIALOG or BRS. These systems add additional operators such as "with" and "near."

The use of the "and" operator serves to narrow a search by looking for entries that contain **both** terms, e.g., North "and" South. The "or" operator serves to enlarge the search by looking for entries that contain **either** of the terms, North "or" South. The "not" search narrows a search by eliminating from the search all citations with the undesired term, North "not" South. The "not" operator should be used with caution as it might eliminate desired entries (see Figure 3.3).

Accessing OPACs via the Internet

Most libraries that have OPACs have a home page on the Internet (World Wide Web). In general the home page gives information about the library, such as its location, hours and services. The home page should be accessible using a web browser. However, if you want to search the catalog itself it is usually necessary to have the ability to **telnet** to the library's catalog. Not all web browsers are initially set to use telnet and that function needs to be installed or activated. If you use AOL it will be necessary to install a program that has a telnet option, such as COMMNET, on your hard drive. Prodigy includes the telnet option. Libraries use different systems for operating their OPAC. Among the most popular vendors are NOTIS, DRA, III, Dynix, and GEAC. Each system has different searching techniques. The general instructions for searching each system can be found by searching for that system name on the Internet. In addition, each library has it's own logon procedure. For example, most libraries that use III use *library* for their logon. To locate the list of libraries using III search the Internet using **III.COM.** On the home page you will find a list of the 600+ libraries using III. In addition, the III home page provides an access point for HYTELNET. If you click on HYTELNET you will get a list of **all** library systems on the Internet. The HYTELNET home page (also accessed by searching http//Iibrary.usask.ca/hytelnet) includes the following menu options: library catalogs arranged geographically, library catalogs arranged by

Figure 3.3

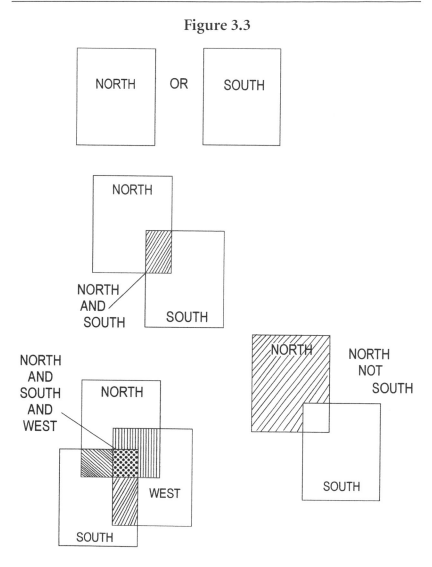

vendor (III, NOTIS, etc.) and help files for library catalogs. The geographical list is divided as follows: The Americas; Europe/Middle East; and Asia/Pacific/South Africa. HYTELNET is maintained by Peter Scott (pscott@library.berkeley.edu). To find information about libraries using NOTIS search www.notis.com. DYNIX and NOTIS are found on the same home page. GEAC is located by searching www.geac.com and DRA information can be found by searching www.dra.com.

Exercises for Chapter 3

1. Do an author search for Jean M. Auel.
   (A) First try just her last name.
   (B) Record (or print) the results.
   (C) Try her full name.
   (D) Was there a difference in the results?
   (E) Was there a difference in the time it took for the system to search?
2. Do a title search for Jean M. Auel's book *Clan of the Cave Bear.*
   (A) Try the search first using just the first word of the title. Record (or print) your results.
   (B) Try the search again using the first couple of words of the title. How did your results differ from previous title search?
3. Suppose you did not know the exact title of the book in question 2 but did know "Cave Bear" was in the title.
   (A) How would you search for this title? Try your solution.
   (B) Did it work? If not, can you give an explanation?
4. Try a subject search for books on cave dwellers.
   (A) What subject did you enter? Was it successful?
   (B) Record (or print) your results. How would you use information from this search to find additional books?
   (C) Call up a complete record from this search. What is its status?
   (D) Does the library have more than one copy? If you are using a public library system, does the system show locations by branch libraries?
5. If the system you are using allows Boolean searching, search Auel *and* Bear.
   (A) Try various combinations of the books by Auel, using various words in the titles. Record (or print) your results.
   (B) Try other combinations that are of interest to you. What did you discover?

Important Terms for Chapter 3

OPAC	*CD-ROM*
keyword	*Boolean operators*
bar code	*network*
LAN	*user friendly*
truncated	*Internet*

Hytelnet	*Telnet*
vendor	*World Wide Web (WWW)*

Important Books for Chapter 3

Crawford, Walt, et al. *Bibliographic Displays in the On-Line Catalog.* Boston: G. K. Hall, 1986.

Dial-In. An annual guide to library on-line public access catalogs in North America. Westport, CT: Meckler, 1991– .

Dictionary of Computing. 3rd ed. New York: Oxford University Press, 1990.

Fayen, Emily G. *The On-Line Catalog: Improving Public Access to Library Materials.* Boston: G. K. Hall, 1983.

Glossbrenner, Alfred. *The Complete Handbook of Personal Computer Communications.* 3rd ed. New York: St. Martin's Press, 1989.

Manual of Online Search Strategies. 2nd ed. New York: Toronto: G. K. Hall; Maxwell Macmillan Canada, 1992.

Matthews, Joseph R. *Access to On-Line Catalogs.* 2nd ed. New York: Neal Schuman, 1985.

OPAC Directory 1994: An Annual Guide to Internet Accessible Online Public Access Catalogs. Westport, Conn.: Meckler, 1994.

Peters, Thomas. *The Online Catalog: A Critical Examination of Public Use.* Jefferson, NC: McFarland, 1991.

4. Subject Headings

Objectives

After studying this chapter the student shall be able to
* use *Library of Congress Subject Headings*
* find correct subject headings for a particular topic
* use various forms of cross references correctly

General Information

Often, students looking for material in the library do not have specific titles or authors in hand and need to use subject headings instead. This is particularly true during the early stages of a search. Frequently, students guess the appropriate heading to use. A proper and specific subject heading is essential for the efficient use of the card catalog, on-line catalog (OPAC), CD-ROM indexes and catalogs, and periodical indexes. Using a heading that seems logical but is inappropriate wastes effort, especially when using OPACs and CD products. For example, searching for information on the battles of the American Civil War, one might use initially the heading **Civil War**. Titles about the Civil War are found more appropriately under **United States — History — Civil War, 1861–1865**.

The dates of events are also important since citations are arranged chronologically within groups. Thus entries **United States — History — Revolution, 1775–1783** and **United States — History — Colonial Period, ca. 1600–1774** both appear before the Civil War entry because they precede it in time. Some catalogs contain cross-references to help minimize this problem. These are of two types: the *see* and the *see also* reference, which lists other closely related subjects.

To help find the correct subject heading when cross-references are not available, searchers need to find additional headings. Users should consult one or more special books that help to discover appropriate subject headings. The most comprehensive of these is *Library of Congress Subject Headings* (LCSH), a four-volume work conspicuous by its bright red cover. Well-equipped libraries use this four-volume work as the "bible" of subject headings and often place this work at the card catalog or near the OPAC terminals. Other books of subject headings that are not as comprehensive are the: *Sears List of Subject Headings; Subject Cross Reference Guide;* and *Cross Reference Index.*

Libraries also may have books of subject headings for *specific indexes or subjects.* For example: *Thesaurus of Sociological Indexing Terms* and *A to Zoo: Subject Access to Children's Picture Books.*

Consulting such works before using the catalog will save time and frustration and may provide additional headings, more specific or descriptive than the headings originally checked. Some headings, particularly in the *Library of Congress* work, may contain voluminous entries, filling an entire column or more. See Figure 4.1 for the subject **Public Opinion Polls** that continues on to a second column in LCSH. This means the subject is very broad and the user might consider specifying a narrower topic. This is particularly important in writing term papers. Problems in writing term papers often begin by selecting topics that are too comprehensive.

Using Library of Congress Subject Headings (LCSH)

The LCSH is the list of subject headings assigned by the Library of Congress to books in its collection. It reflects the changes and growth in the collection since the development of the LC Classification system in 1898. The 14th edition was published in 1991 and is the first edition to use abbreviations introduced with computer thesaurus in the mid–1980s. The 21st edition was published in 1998. The introductory material in the front of Volume 1 contains explanations and instruction on how headings are arranged and assigned.

Figure 4.1
Library of Congress Subject Headings

War, 1939-1945—Public opinion;
United States—History—Civil War,
1861-1865—Foreign public opinion;
and subdivision Foreign public
opinion *under names of countries,*
etc.
- NT Block wardens (Local government)
  Knowledge, Sociology of
  Mass media and public opinion
  Polemics
  Rumor
  Scale analysis (Psychology)
  Social pressure
— **Jews**
Here are entered works on public opinion of
Jews. Works dealing with public opinion about
Jews are entered under Jews—Public opinion.
— **Research**
  USE Public opinion polls
Public opinion and mass media
  USE Mass media and public opinion
Public opinion polls
  ⌜HM261⌝
Here are entered works on the technique of public
opinion polling. Works on polls on a specific subject
are entered under the appropriate heading for the
topic with the subdivision Public opinion. Works on
such polls taken in a specific place are assigned an
additional heading Public opinion—⌜place⌝. Works
on such polls limited to a specific class of persons are
assigned an additional heading for the group of peo-
ple with the subdivision Attitudes.
  UF Opinion polls
    Polls
    Public opinion—Research
    Public opinion research
    Straw votes
  BT Social surveys
  RT Market surveys
  NT Election forecasting
— **Computer programs**
— **Law and legislation** *(May Subd Geog)*
Public opinion research
  USE Public opinion polls
Public order
  USE Public policy (Law)
Public ownership
  USE Government ownership
    Municipal ownership
Public ownership of close corporations
  USE Going public (Securities)
Public peace (Landfriede)
  USE Landfriede
Public personnel management
  USE Civil service—Personnel management
Public places
  USE Public spaces
Public playgrounds
  USE Playgrounds
Public policy
  USE *subdivision* Government policy *under*
    subjects; and headings of the type
    ⌜Topic⌝ *and state and* ⌜Topic⌝
    policy, e.g. Science and state;
    Economic policy

Public policy management
  USE Policy sciences
Public printing
  USE Printing, Public
Public procurement
  USE Government purchasing
Public property
  USE Government property
Public prosecutors *(May Subd Geog)*
  UF District attorneys
    Prosecutors, Public
  BT Government attorneys
  NT Informations
    Lay prosecutors
    Promoters of justice (Canon law)
    Special prosecutors
— **Education** *(May Subd Geog)*
  BT Law—Study and teaching
Public purchasing
  USE Government purchasing
Public radio *(May Subd Geog)*
  UF Non-commercial radio
    Noncommercial radio
  BT Public broadcasting
    Radio broadcasting
  RT Radio programs, Public service
— **Law and legislation** *(May Subd Geog)*
Public records *(May Subd Geog)*
Here are entered works on public records in gen-
eral, including those held in courthouses. Court re-
cord books containing short case summaries and
judgments, as well as works on the administrative
records of courts, are entered under Court records.
  UF Government records
  BT Public administration
    Records
  RT Archives
    Government information
  SA *subdivision* Public records *under*
    names of individual government
    agencies
  NT Automobile drivers' records
    County government—Records and
      correspondence
    Court records
    Government correspondence
    Government paperwork
    Memorandums
    Municipal government—Records and
      correspondence
    Police—Records and correspondence
    Public land records
    Social security records
— **Access control**
  ⌜CD986.5⌝
  BT Privacy, Right of
— **Law and legislation** *(May Subd Geog)*
— **Preservation**
  USE Archives
Public relations *(May Subd Geog)*
  ⌜HD59-HD59.6 (Management)⌝
  ⌜HM263 (Social psychology)⌝

Subject headings may be one word or several words. A one word subject heading is usually a noun, with concepts using the singular form and objects using plural forms:

> authorship (concept — singular)
> soils (object — plural)

Two word headings are generally an adjective and a noun and may be inverted, especially if the adjective describes a language or a nationality. In recent years the natural word order is the preferred form except for language, national or ethnic adjectives. Older headings are more likely to be in inverted word order. Examples are:

> authorship, disputed
> coach horses
> churches, Anglican
> Camsa language
> dramatists, Italian
> public records (see Figure 4.1)

Names of geographic places are usually inverted to put the significant word first, e.g., Michigan, Lake. Headings with more than two words may include conjunctions and prepositional phrases. Headings with reciprocal relations or generally used associated ideas may be combined. Those headings with prepositional phrases may be in the *inverted format*. Examples are:

> charity laws and legislation
> bites and stings
> Antietam, Battle of, 1862
> bachelor of arts degree
> technology and civilization

Place names may also be used as subject headings and subheadings. Over the years the format for place names has changed as have the rules to assign subject headings for place names. In addition, many places have changed their names. Thus place names in card catalogs and even in OPACs are inconsistent and diligent searching is necessary to locate all desired information. An example of a geographic heading that is confusing for users of any type of the catalog is George, Lake (not Lake

George) but Lake George Region. Examples of place name changes include colonies that have become independent nations and changed their name, territories conquered in war resulting in city or country name changes, name changes in cities when governments change such as St. Petersburg-Petrograd-Leningrad, a city known by three different names this century. In 1991, the citizens voted to change the name back to St. Petersburg.

Cross references are always helpful in directing students from incorrect headings to correct headings. Also helpful are cross references between similar headings or between broad and narrow headings. Many libraries, catalogs, and indexes are see and see also headings. The see reference directs the student from an incorrect heading to a correct heading. The 20th edition of LCSH and many computer thesauri have substituted the term use for see. The function remains the same, directing the user to the correct heading.

The see also (or SA) reference directs the student to other headings that are related. Recent computer thesauri and LCSH are supplementing the see also reference with additional breakdowns as follows:

> RT = related term
> BT = broader term
> NT =narrower term
> UF = use from, a cross reference from the *use* reference

The inclusion of the UF in a list means that terms designated with UF are *not* good subject headings and should not be used when searching.

In Figure 4.1 for the subject heading **Public opinion polls,** note that UF references include *Opinion polls; Polls; Public Opinion-Research; Public opinion research, and Straw votes.* For the subject heading **Public records,** note that the UF reference is *Government records.* These headings are not to be used and if the user looked, for example, under *Opinion polls* LCSH says *USE Public opinion polls.* The BT or broader terms for the subject heading **Public records** include *Public administration and Records.* The RT or related terms are *Archives and Government information.* The note for SA (see also) says *"subdivision* Public records *under names of individual government agencies."* The list for NT or narrower terms includes 10 headings, ranging from *Automobile drivers' records to Social security records.* For examples of a use reference see Figure 4.1 *Public records-Preservation USE Archive* and for *Public ownership USE Government ownership; Municipal ownership.*

LCSH also includes a variety of notes with the subject headings and their subdivisions. Often the beginning or subject class number (see Chapter 2) of the call number is included. See Figure 4.1 **Public opinion polls** and note the call number HM261. Also note that there are call numbers included with some of the subdivisions, (see Figure 4. 1) e.g. **Public records-Access control** is CD986.5. With this information the student can go to the shelves and browse to see which books the library has on the subject. Having part of the call number is also useful with those OPACs that have a call number browse search option. Another type of note that may be included is a scope note-one that explains what is included or excluded in that particular subject heading. See Figure 4.1 for **Public records,** note that this heading says (May *Subd Geog*) and includes a scope note that begins "Here are entered works on public records in general, including those held in courthouses. Court record books...

There are generally four types of subdivisions used by the Library of Congress:

1. topical — ones that limit the concept
   semiconductors — failures
2. form — includes the literary form
   addresses, essays, lectures
   periodical
   abstracts
   collected works (Figure 4.1)
3. chronological — shows time period(s)
   Sicily — civilization —15th century
   Sri Lanka — history —1505–1948
4. geographical — shows places
   public buildings — Spain

The countries that are exceptions to this rule are the United States, Canada, Russia and Great Britain. These countries have more specific breakdowns, using names of states, provinces, regions, constituent countries and republics instead of just the name of the country, e.g. public buildings — Washington, D.C.

Not all possible subdivisions are listed in LCSH. Subdivisions are marked by a dash that eliminates the need to repeat the main heading. If a subdivision has a subdivision there will be two dashes.

Searching the Catalog

If you are searching the subject heading in the card catalog you can browse easily through the cards and find singular and plural forms of the term and other headings beginning with the same word. Subject cards can be identified from other cards in the catalog because the topmost line on the card is typed in capital letters or in red ink. In most OPACs a user starts a subject search fro the menu or with a command s= or su=. If you are subject searching in an OPAC instead of in a card catalog the process may be more difficult, depending on the system used. Some OPACs allow free text searching (see Chapter 3). In others the subject term entered into the computer must be an *exact* match to a Library of Congress subject heading. Problems could be singular vs. plural forms of the word, inverted terms, etc. Searching any catalog by subject is limited by the number of subject terms assigned and by the imprecise use of some headings and the changes in terminology through time.

Exercises for Chapter 4

1. Using *Library of Congress Subject Headings,* look up the subject **Last Supper.** Record call number, any notes, cross references, subheadings or other subjects beginning with the term **Last Supper.**
2. Using *Library of Congress Subject Headings* find the correct subject heading(s) needed to locate information about the conflicts between the Jews and the Palestinians and or other Arab groups.
3. Using *Library of Congress Subject Headings* locate and record one or two examples of subject headings that use or contain the following:
   (A) chronological subdivisions
   (B) geographical subdivisions
   (C) scope note(s)
   (D) class note(s)
   (E) multiple cross references
4. Using your example in question 3E, trace and record all cross references to BT, NT, RT, SA, UF and USE. Is the example in 3E a topic usable for a term paper? Why or why not?

Important Terms in Chapter 4

cross reference	"RT" reference
"see" reference	"USE" reference
"see also" reference	"UF" reference
"BT" reference	OPAC
"NT" reference	LCSH

Important Books for Chapter 4

Atkins, Thomas V. *Cross Reference Index: A Guide to Search Terms*. New York: Bowker, 1984, 1989.

Booth, Barbara, and Michael Blair. *Thesaurus of Sociological Indexing Terms*. 4th ed. San Diego, CA, 1996.

Lima, Carolyn W., and John A. Lima. *"A to Zoo" Subject Access to Children's Picture Books*. 4th ed. New York R. R. Bowker, 1993.

Markey, Karen. *Subject Searching in Library Catalogs Before and After the Introduction of On-Line Catalogs*. Dublin, OH: OCLC On-Line Corp., 1984.

Sears List of Subject Headings. 15th ed. New York: N. W. Wilson, 1994.

Subject Guide to Books in Print. 5 vols. Thesaurus. New York: R. R. Bowker, 1997–98.

Thesaurus of Psychological Index Terms. 8th ed. Alvin Walker, ed. Arlington, VA: American Psychological Association, 1997.

United States. Library of Congress. Subject Cataloging Division. *Library of Congress Subject Headings*. 21st ed. 1998.

5. Bibliography

Objectives

After studying this chapter the student shall be able to
- distinguish between the two types of bibliography, book length and short lists
- figure out where to find lists of available published books and how to use these lists
- use the *National Union Catalog*, the *Cumulative Book Index* and the *Bibliographic Index* to locate materials
- distinguish between annotated bibliographies and the other types and how to find materials in them
- recognize an appropriate format for writing bibliographies
- locate bibliographies on specific topics

General Information

After defining a topic the writer will find a bibliography an essential part of research. *Webster's Third New International Dictionary of the English Language Unabridged* (1971) defines bibliography as follows:

> 1a: the history, identification, or analytical and systematic description or classification of writings or publications considered as material objects b: the investigation or determination of the relationships of varying texts or multiple editions of a single work or a related group of works — called

also *analytic bibliography, descriptive bibliography.* **2 :** a list or catalog, often descriptive or critical notes, of writings related to a particular subject, period or author «a *b—* of modern poetry» «a *b—* of the 17th century»; *also* a list of works *b—* of Walt Whitman» «a publisher's *b—*»**3 :** the works, or a list of them, mentioned in a text or consulted by an author in a production of that text — usu. Included as an appendix to the work «a *b—* of 40 books and articles» **4 :** the study of bibliography or bibliographic methods «an intensive course in *b—*»

Most students are familiar with bibliographies that are citations of the works used by an author in writing a book or paper (see definition 3 above). Yet, bibliographies such as those found in definition 2 are extremely useful to the sophisticated searcher. Libraries have many bibliographies of this type that are invaluable when preparing a list of materials on a topic.

Bibliographies may be book length, containing thousands of entries, or may be only several pages in length. For instance, the *Indians of North and South America* by Carolyn Wolf is a comprehensive bibliography containing over 4,200 sources of information on that topic.

On the other hand, some bibliographies are listings of the works by a particular author, some *about* a particular author and some are both. For example the bibliography by Joan Crane, *Willa Cather: A Bibliography*, is just a list of works by Willa Cather. Yet the bibliography by John A. Stoler, *Daniel Defoe: An Annotated Bibliography of Modern Criticism, 1900–1980*, contains a list of works by Defoe *and* a list of critical analysis of Defoe's works. To find these bibliographies in the card catalog one looks under the author's name as a subject. The author's name will be typed in red ink or printed in capital letters. When using an OPAC the student must do a subject search.

Other bibliographies are topical. Subjects or authors' names will be arranged alphabetically. Sometimes the student will find bibliographies that contain both subjects and authors in one alphabetical listing. Another category of bibliographies is determined by geographical area. Some of these contain items about or published in a specific country, while others may be regional or international in scope. Further, a distinction may be made on the time period with which the bibliography deals. For instance, a bibliography might contain only works of Russian authors of the 19th century.

Some bibliographies are detailed lists of other bibliographies. A

Asking the librarian for assistance can be a time saver.

logical starting point for researching a particular topic is to consult one of these comprehensive bibliographies. Then one should see if the library has or can obtain the most useful ones. There is an extensive section in the catalog under the subject bibliography that lists most of the bibliographies in the library.

Also, bibliographies can be located under a specific subject heading that has the subheading "bibliography"—for example, air pollution–bibliography contains references to lists of information on air pollution.

The following are books that are either bibliographies or contain useful information about bibliographies.

Books in Print

Books in Print (BIP in library lingo) is a current list of books published by *major* American publishers. Students will find a set in all libraries, book stores and other large stores with a book department.

BIP is a listing of books *available for purchase*. This listing could include a book written 50 years ago if it is still available for purchase from the publisher. A book published a year ago that is no longer available for purchase will not be listed. BIP is published annually and the new edition generally is available in the fall.

Books in Print includes scholarly, popular, adult, juvenile, reprint editions and all other types of books, provided they are published or exclusively distributed in the United States and are available to the trade or to the public for single or multiple copy purchase according to the preface to BIP.

BIP has author, title, subject and publisher sections arranged alphabetically. The subject section, *Subject Guide to Books in Print*, is useful in preparing a list of books on a specific topic. The author section is a listing of the authors found in the subject section and the title section is a listing of the titles in the subject section. The publisher volume is a directory of included publishers.

The entries in BIP include the author(s) name(s), title, publisher, date of publication, price of the book, and other ordering information for libraries and book stores. The ordering information is primarily useful for library staff but may be used by the student to order books directly from the publisher.

Library of Congress Catalog of Printed Cards *and the* National Union Catalog

The *Library of Congress Catalog of Printed Cards*, commonly called the *LC Cat*, was first published in 1942 and covered the period 1898 (when cards were first printed) to 1942. Supplements in monthly, quarterly, annual and five-year accumulations have appeared since. The *LC Cat* is a reproduction of the author cards printed by the Library of Congress. The *LC Cat* is not a complete list of books at the Library of Congress because the library has books for which cards have never been printed.

Many major libraries in the United States and Canada have supplied the Library of Congress with cards of local, unusual or foreign publications that they have added to their collections. The Library of Congress has interfiled these cards with the cards they have printed, and have thus maintained a "National Union [Card] Catalog" in their Washington, D.C. main building. Each library supplying information has a letter code and the code is added to the card supplied to the Library of Congress. When several libraries supply the same information, the code for each library is added.

In 1956 the Library of Congress changed the scope of the *LC Cat* to include all the entries supplied by other libraries. The title was changed to *National Union Catalog*, NUC for short, to reflect the change in scope. The codes for all the libraries supplying information are printed after the entry. This helps to locate libraries having a copy of a particular book, which may then be borrowed through interlibrary loan (see Chapter 14).

In 1968 a commercial publisher, Mansell, began a major undertaking, the printing of the *National Union Catalog, Pre-1956 Imprints*. This catalog lists in one alphabet all the cards printed by the Library of Congress from 1898 to 1956 and all the cards supplied by other libraries up to 1965. All three categories, *LC Cat, NUC,* and *NUC Pre-56 Imprints* are primarily author listings.

In 1950 the Library of Congress began printing a subject approach to *LC Cat* called *Library of Congress, Books — Subjects*. It is published quarterly with annual and five-year accumulations and is arranged by the subject headings assigned to each book by the Library of Congress. The last cumulative set is 1970 to 1974. Annual volumes continued until 1982. Beginning in 1983 the microfiche NUC contains both authors and subjects in one alphabet.

The Library of Congress now contributes all its new entries to OCLC's main database. The National Library of Canada also contributes its new entries to OCLC's main database. All OCLC members contribute their holding to World Cat (main database) making it an extremely comprehensive online bibliography.

Cumulative Book Index

The *Cumulative Book Index* (CBI) is an author-title-subject world list of books published in English. It also includes some government documents, pamphlets and privately published items. All entries are in a single alphabetical list. The entries include the author(s), title, publisher, date of publication, price and other information for ordering from the publisher. See Figure 5.1 for a sample entry. Note the many

Figure 5.1 Cumulative Book Index

Ireland, Kenneth F.
A classical introduction to modern number theory; [by] Kenneth Ireland, Michael Rosen. 2nd ed (Graduate texts in mathematics, 84) 389p 1990 Springer-Verlag (NY)
ISBN 0-387-97329-X   LC 90-9848

Ireland

Antiquities, Celtic
Laing, L. R. Celtic Britain and Ireland, AD200-800. £32.50 1990 Irish Acad. Press

Civilization
Weisser, H. Hippocrene companion guide to Ireland. $14.95 1990 Hippocrene Bks.

Description and travel
Clark, W. Sailing round Ireland. 2nd ed pa £7.95 1990 North-West Bks.
O'Farrell, P. By rail through the heart of Ireland. pa £7.95 1990 Mercier Press
Distr. in USA by Dufour Eds. pa $16.95
Weisser, H. Hippocrene companion guide to Ireland. $14.95 1990 Hippocrene Bks.

Views
Browne, F. The genius of Father Browne. 1990 Wolfhound Press
Distr. in USA by Dufour Eds. $40

Emigration and immigration
Migrations. 1990 Wolfhound Press
Distr. in USA by Dufour Eds. $26

Genealogy
Directories
A Guide to Irish churches and graveyards. 1990 Genealogical

History
To 1172
Hall, R. Viking age archaeology in Britain and Ireland. pa £3.50 1990 Shire Publs.
Laing, L. R. Celtic Britain and Ireland, AD200-800. £32.50 1990 Irish Acad. Press

20th century
Dunleavy, J. E. Douglas Hyde. 1991 University of Calif. Press (Berkeley)

Politics and government
1901-1910
Allen, K. The politics of James Connolly. £16.50 1990 Pluto Press

1910-1921
Allen, K. The politics of James Connolly. £16.50 1990 Pluto Press

Social life and customs
20th century
Donleavy, J. P. A singular country. $18.95 1990 Norton

Irigaray, Luce
Marine lover of Friedrich Nietzsche; translated by Gillian C. Gill. 190p $35 1991 Columbia Univ. Press
ISBN 0-231-07082-9   LC 90-27059

subheadings under the subject **Ireland**. Note that author entries and title entries are interfiled with the subject.

Bibliographic Index

The *Bibliographic Index* is a bibliography of bibliographies. It is a list of bibliographies arranged by subject and where they may be found. If, for example the student desires a bibliography on prehistoric agriculture, it may be found under that subject, **Agriculture, Prehistoric**. See Figure 5.2 for an example of what the reference looks like. The bibliographies included in *Bibliographic Index* may be a complete book length listing or a bibliography after a journal article, book or chapter of a book.

Annotated Bibliographies

Certain bibliographies are annotated — that is, they describe the books included. Some of these are lists of reference works with annotations. All libraries have bibliographies of this type and it is essential to consult them to find the best reference books on a subject.

The *Guide to Reference Books*, edited by Robert Balay (11th edition, 1996), is an excellent example and is available in all libraries. Students will find it useful to read the few introductory pages in the front of the

Figure 5.2   Bibliographic Index

volume. Other similar guides are available; some are general, like the *Guide to Reference Books*, and others cover only specific subjects such as astronomy or American history. A few of these guides have been published in inexpensive paperback and would be a useful addition to any student's personal library. See the list after this chapter for additional examples.

After looking at the examples in Figures 5.1 and 5.2 and completing the exercises after this chapter the student will have discovered that there are many different formats for bibliographies. When preparing a bibliography of one's own for an assignment, a specific format may be desired. The sensible way to decide the appropriate format is to ask the teacher if he or she has any preference. Most formats include the information in generally the same order shown here, but punctuation and spacing and other details differ.

Author (last name first). *Title*, edition number. Place of Publication: Name of Publisher, date of publication.

The most important thing to remember is to be consistent, using the same order, punctuation and spacing throughout the bibliography.

Listed below are some popular term paper guides and style sheets. They all give instruction for, and examples of, bibliographic format. Additionally these guides provide invaluable information to the term paper writer, and all students should own one.

Term Paper Guides (see also Chapter 16)

The Chicago Manual of Style, 14th ed. Chicago: University of Chicago Press, 1993.

Fleischer, Eugene B. *A Style Manual for Citing Microfilm and Non-Print Media*. Chicago: American Library Association, 1978.

MLA Handbook for Writers of Research Papers, Theses and Dissertations, 4th ed. Edited by Joseph Gibaldi and Walter S. Achtert, New York: Modern Language Association, 1995.

Thurston, Marjorie H., and Eugene S. Wright. *The Preparation of Term Papers and Reports*, 6th ed. Minneapolis: Burgess Publishing Company, 1970.

Turabian, Kate L. *Manual for Writers of Term Papers, Theses and Dissertations*. 6th ed. Chicago: University of Chicago Press, 1996.

VanLeunen, Mary-Claire. *A Handbook for Scholars.* 2nd ed. New York: Alfred A. Knopf, 1992.

Exercises for Chapter 5

1. Find the bibliographies in your library for the two authors listed below. Answer the questions about both authors. If you have problems using the catalog or locating the books on the shelves, ask the librarian.
   (A) Edgar Allan Poe (see the subject card or choose subject on the OPAC menu POE, EDGAR ALLAN 1809–1849 — BIBLIOGRAPHY):
      1. How many bibliographies does your library have on Poe?
      2. In what section of the library are the bibliographies located?
      3. Are the bibliographies of works *about* Poe, of works *by* Poe, or both?
      4. Do any of these bibliographies circulate?
   (B) D. H. Lawrence (See subject card or choose subject on the OPAC menu LAWRENCE, DAVID HERBERT 1885–1930 — BIBLIOGRAPHY):
      1. How many bibliographies does your library have on Lawrence?
      2. In what section of the library are the bibliographies located?
      3. Are the bibliographies of works *about* Lawrence, of works *by* Lawrence, or both?
      4. Do any of these bibliographies circulate?
2. Read the preface to BIP, CBI and *LC Cat.*
   (A) Using the **author** section of BIP:
      1. Count and record the number of entries for Dean R. Koontz.
      2. What information is provided about each book?
   (B) Using CBI for 1989:
      1. Count and record the number of entries for Stephen King.
      2. What information is provided in each entry?
      3. Does this information differ from BIP? If so, how?
   (C) Using NUC (**authors**), check the 1973–1977 accumulation for Stephen King.
      1. Count and record the number of entries.
      2. Check annual volumes or microfiche edition, if available.
      3. How do the entries differ from those in CBI and BIP?

3. The following questions are based on Princess Diana as a subject.
   (A) Using the *Subject Guide to Books in Print*, count and record the number of entries.
   (B) Using the last five years of CBI, count and record the number of entries.
   (C) Under what heading(s) would you look for information about Princess Diana in a guide to reference books?
   (D) Check WorldCat using subject and word and search for Princess Diana. Also search using Princess of Wales. Record your results.
   (E) Which of the sources checked provided the best information?

Important Terms in Chapter 5

BIP	*Books-Subjects*
NUC	*LC Cat*
CBI	*Bibliography of Bibliographies*

This chapter has described only a few bibliographies that can be useful in identifying materials not located by using the catalog. The following list includes these plus a few more. Libraries will have many more bibliographies than those listed below. They may be found by using the subject approach to the catalog and by asking the reference librarian.

Important Books for Chapter 5

American Reference Books Annual, 1970– , ed. by Bohdan S. Wynar. Littleton, CO: Libraries Unlimited, 1970– .

Balay, Robert. *Guide to Reference Books*, 11th ed. Chicago: American Library Association, 1996.

Besterman, Theodore. *A World Bibliography of Bibliographies and of Bibliographical Catalogues, Calendars, Abstracts, Digests, Indexes and the Like*. 4th ed., revised and greatly enlarged. Lausanne, Switzerland: Societas Bibliographica, 1965–1966. 5 vols.

Bibliographic Index: A Cumulative Bibliography of Bibliographies, 1937– . New York: H. W. Wilson, 1938– .

Books in Print: An Author-Title Series Index to the "Publishers' Trade List Annual," 1948– . New York: R. R. Bowker, 1948– .

British Museum. Department of Printed Books. *General Catalogue of Printed Books.* Photolithographic edition to 1955. London: Trustees of the British Museum, 1959–66. 263 vols. (Supplements, 1956–1965, 1966–1970, 1971–1975, 1976–1985, 1986–1987, 1988–1989.)

Cumulative Book Index. New York: H. W. Wilson, 1928– .

National Union Catalog: A Cumulative Author List Representing Library of Congress Printed Cards and Titles Reported by Other American Libraries, 1953–1957. Ann Arbor, MI: Edwards, 1958. 28 vols. (5 year accumulations from 1958–1977.)

National Union Catalog, Pre–1956 Imprints: A Cumulative Author List Representing Library of Congress Printed Cards and Titles Reported by Other American Libraries. London: Mansell, 1968– . (610 vols.)

Subject Guide to Books in Print: An Index to the "Publishers' Trade List Annual," 1957– . New York: R. R. Bowker, 1957– .

United States. Library of Congress. *A Catalog of Books Represented by Library of Congress Printed Cards, Issued to July 31, 1942.* Ann Arbor, MI: Edwards, 1942–1946. 167 vols. (Supplements cover years 1942–1952.)

Walford, Albert John. *Walford's Guide to Reference Materials,* 5th ed. London: Library Association, 1980– . (Vol. 1, 1989, v. 2 1989, v. 3 1991.)

6. Book Reviews and the Parts of a Book

Objectives

After studying this chapter the student shall be able to
- find book reviews using available sources
- identify and use the different parts of a book

Book Reviews

After compiling a list of books on a topic, students may want to choose only several relevant ones for the term paper or other project. There are many types of book review sources and not all libraries will have all the sources.

Most books are reviewed in newspapers and periodicals. The trick is to find the appropriate review for a specific book. Some professional journals contain no articles, just book reviews. Some examples of these are *Choice, New York Review of Books*, and *Booklist*. Other journals, such as *Library Journal and Publishers Weekly*, include many reviews as well as articles covering many topics. Specialized periodicals such as *Journal of American History* review books only in that specialty.

Newspapers often include book reviews. The *New York Times* is the most useful source of newspaper book reviews. It includes book reviews in its daily paper besides the Book Review Section of the Sunday edition. Reviews appearing in the *New York Times* may be located by using the *New York Times Index* under the subject heading book reviews. There is a list of the books reviewed arranged alphabetically by the author's last name. Anthologies — collections of works by many authors, usually poems or short stories — are reviewed and listed alphabetically by the title and found after the author list. The *New York Times Index* shows the date of the review, then page number of the edition and the column number of that page. Roman numerals or letters identify the section number of the edition. A typical listing follows:

Ja	6	III (or B)	19:	3
[month:	[day]	[section]	[page]	[column]
January]				

The most efficient process for finding book reviews is to use the indexes to periodicals. Some of these indexes specialize in book reviews, for example; *Book Review Index, Index to Book Reviews in the Humanities, Book Review Index to Social Science Periodicals* and *Current Book Review Citations.* Most libraries own at least one of the above titles. These indexes list the source of the book review, title of the periodical, volume number, date and pages. Figure 6.1 from *Book Review Index* is a list of reviews. Seventeen books by Dick King-Smith are listed and one to five reviews are included for each title. The titles of the journals containing the reviews are abbreviated and the student must check the abbreviations list at the front of the volume to get the full title of each journal. Another useful source is *Book Review Digest*, which began publishing in 1905 and is issued monthly with annual accumulations. The *Book Review Digest* includes excerpts from reviews besides listing the location of the reviews in journals. It also includes the number of words in the review — which can be a vital clue to its scope (see Figure 6.2). The introductory page to *Book Review Digest* informs how selections for inclusions are made. To find reviews in professional or specialized journals it is necessary to consult the periodicals indexes for that field. For further discussion of periodical indexes see chapters 8 and 9.

To locate a book review use the index for the year the book was originally written, not a reprint date. If the review is not located in that year, check the following year, as reviews will appear up to a year or more after the publication date. Not all sources of book reviews include all books and it may be necessary to consult several sources before locating a review.

Figure 6.1 Book Review Index

King Horn - *King Horn (Allen)*
Specu - v65 - Jl '90 - p564
King-Smith, Dick - *Ace: The Very Important Pig (Illus. by Lynette Hemmant)*
c HB - v66 - S '90 - p602
c KR - v58 - Jl 15 '90 - p1004
c PW - v237 - Je 29 '90 - p102
Alice and Flower and Foxianna (Illus. by John Sharp)
c GP - v28 - S '89 - p5229
Babe: The Gallant Pig (Illus. by Mary Rayner)
c BL - v86 - N 1 '89 - p564
Beware of the Bull! (Illus. by John Sharp)
c GP - v28 - S '89 - p5229
Dodos Are Forever (Illus. by David Parkins)
c BFYC - v25 - Spring '90 - p21
c JB - v53 - D '89 - p279
c Sch Lib - v38 - F '90 - p19
E.S.P.
c Bks for Keeps - S '89 - p9
The Fox Busters
c GP - v29 - My '90 - p5356
The Fox Busters. Audio Version
c BW - v20 - Je 24 '90 - p8
Friends and Brothers.
c Bks for Keeps - My '90 - p13
The Hodgeheg. Audio Version
c TES - D 22 '89 - p26
The Jenius (Illus. by Peter Firmin)
c KR - v58 - Je 15 '90 - p877
c SLJ - v36 - S '90 - p206
Martin's Mice (Illus. by Jez Alborough)
c Par - v64 - D '89 - p229
Martin's Mice. Audio Version
c Sch Lib - v38 - My '90 - p64
Sophie's Snail (Illus. by Claire Minter-Kemp)
c CBRS - v18 - Mr '90 - p90
c CCB-B - v43 - Ja '90 - p112
c HB - v66 - Ja '90 - p89
c HB Guide - v1 - Jl '89 p66
c SLJ - v35 - D '89 - p83
The Toby Man (Illus. by Ian Newsham)
c JB - v54 - F '90 - p27
The Trouble with Edward (Illus. by Jacqui Thomas)
c GP - v28 - N '89 - p5245
c TES - F 2 '90 - p76
Kingdon, Jonathan - *Island Africa*
Nature - v345 - My 24 '90 - p303
New Sci - v127 - S 22 '90 - p66
TLS - Je 29 '90 - p707

Parts of a Book

Most books consist of a title page, preface, introduction, text and appendixes. Each of these parts contains useful information. Knowing where to find this information is helpful.

The title page (usually the first page with printing) gives the following information: (a) title of the book, (b) author(s), (c) publishing company, (d) place of publication, and sometimes (e) the date of publication. The back (or "verso") of the title page also contains useful information. It usually includes a copyright notice (name of the owner and a date frequently with the symbol ©) and sometimes edition and printing information (e.g., 2nd edition, 3rd printing; no such statement usually means it is a first edition). Recently publishers have also included cataloging information including subject headings. The ISBN (International Standard Book Number) identifies the publisher in a prefix (this publisher's is 0-89950-) and the actual book is the digits following (e.g., this book is 895-2). The ISBN number is used not only for ordering books from the publisher, but as a unique identifier of that book, that edition, etc., among a possible group of very similar titled books. The ISBN is also used as a search key in OPACs, OCLC and other databases.

Most nonfiction books have a preface where the author explains

Figure 6.2   Book Review Digest

BLACKBURN, ROBIN, 1940-. The making of New World slavery; from the Baroque to the Creole. 602p $35 1997 Verso Eds.
   306.3   1. Slavery—America
   ISBN 1-85984-890-7   LC 96-45603

SUMMARY: "In his companion volume to The Overthrow of Colonial Slavery (1988), Blackburn . . . traces the development of slavery in the New World. He argues that independent traders and businessmen intent on capitalizing on the birth of consumer societies were the driving force behind the rise of the Atlantic slave trade and the sustenance of the plantation system. Thus, although early-modern European states endorsed and profited from slavery, private commercial interests are held primarily responsible for the cruelties of slave traffic and the inhumane conditions of the plantation. . . . [The author argues that] an emerging racial consciousness was used to legitimize New World slavery and [explains] how the plantation contributed to the industrial and military success of the United States and Europe." (Libr J) Index.

REVIEW: Economist v343 p5 Je 21 '97 (850w)
"Mr Blackburn, an honest and reasonable historian, has kept his head admirably. . . . Mr Blackburn's command, also admirable, ranges from statistics about the slave trade to the kind of music which survived on the plantations, and includes some extremely well-chosen illustrations. No comparable history pulls together so much recent work on the economy and ideology of early modern slavery, or consistently maintains such a sure and honourable tone in its narration."

REVIEW: Libr J v122 p118 Ja '97. Raymond J. Palin (150w)

REVIEW: Nation v264 p25 Mr 31 '97. Eric Foner (1850w)
"[This] is the second installment in a magnificent work of contemporary scholarship. . . . Blackburn's account draws on his remarkable command of the voluminous literature on slavery that has appeared in the past two generations. He is sensitive to subtle differences between slave systems. . . . As in his previous work, he situates the rise of slavery in the context of the major European powers' internal histories."

REVIEW: New Statesman (Engl) v126 p44 Mr 14 '97. Ziauddin Sardar (1250w)

REVIEW: Times Lit Suppl no4909 p3 My 2 '97. Anthony Pagden (2750w)
"[This is an] impressive new study. . . . [It] is an exhaustive, powerfully written and compelling book, even if it is also at times quirky and fragmentary and sometimes buries the narrative beneath an excess of detail. It covers, as no other study has ever done, all the major European slave societies in the Americas and almost every conceivable aspect of their melancholy story. Together with Blackburn's earlier work in this area, . . . it provides the best account we have not only of what is still the most dismal chapter in the history of man's inhumanity to man, but also of the place of an often overlooked institution in the evolution of the modern European state system."

BLACKMORE, SUSAN J., 1951-. In search of the light; the adventures of a parapsychologist; [by] Susan Blackmore. [Rev ed] 286p pa $16.95 1996 Prometheus Bks.
   133.8   1. Parapsychology 2. Blackmore, Susan J., 1951-
   ISBN 1-57392-061-4 (pa)   LC 96-16260

SUMMARY: "Most of this book repeats the author's earlier The Adventures of a Parapsychologist; a final group of chapters brings the story up to date. . . . Initially involved in Tarot card reading, and then in various patterns of parapsychological research in which others had claimed to find evidence of psi (psychic functioning), [Blackmore] repeatedly found no such evidence in her own experience. Gradually becoming skeptical of other studies, she shifted her own research to topics of similar interest (such as out-of-body experiences and near-death experiences) studied in ways compatible with the general framework of current science." (Choice) Bibliography. Index.

REVIEW: Choice v34 p691 D '96. I.L. Child (180w)
"Blackmore, a young English woman, early formed an expectation that parapsychology could provide a life pursuit of great promise for understanding the fundamental nature of humanity. She tells the story in terms of personal relationships in which she has engaged in this vein. . . . In recent years, she has still been able to sustain her skepticism, but considers new kinds of evidence more challenging than earlier ones. A well-written, interesting life history. General; undergraduate through faculty."

REVIEW: Sci Books Films v33 p36 Mr '97. Paul J. Rosch (500w)
"This book recounts the author's enthusiasm and belief in paranormal phenomena while at Oxford, where she received a degree in psychology and physiology. She subsequently went on to obtain a Ph.D. in parapsychology from the University of Surrey. . . . The revelations contained in this chatty autobiographical narrative are intriguing and will appeal to anyone with a remote interest in any aspect of this topic. The book is written for the average reader; those with greater experience and knowledge in the field may argue that much has been omitted or that certain terms—such as the discussion of psi, which makes no distinction between paranormal cognition (psi-gamma) and paranormal action (psi-kappa or expressive psi)—are not carefully explained. . . . Interest in this subject is not likely to wane, and those wishing to embark on a similar quest should read this personal account to avoid attempting to 'reinvent the wheel.'"

BLOOM, HAROLD, 1930-, ed. Charlotte Brontë's Jane Eyre.
See Charlotte Brontë's Jane Eyre

BLOOM, VALERIE, 1956-. Fruits; a Caribbean counting poem; illustrated by David Axtell. col il $15.95 1997 Holt & Co.
   811   1. Children's poetry 2. Counting
   ISBN 0-8050-5171-6   LC 96-28890

SUMMARY: This is a poem "about a young Jamaican girl who teaches her little sister the joys of sneaking, hoarding, and chowing down on luscious island fruits. 'One fe you a find!/ De smaddy who lef dem really kind./ One fe you an' six fe me./ If you want more, climb de tree.' Gluttony takes its toll though, and in the end big sister moans, 'Ten banana, mek dem stay,/ Ah feelin' really full today./ Mek me lie down on me bed, quick./ Lawd, ah feelin' really sick.' . . . Ages four to seven." (Bull Cent Child Books)

REVIEW: Booklist v93 p1244 Mr 15 '97. Karen Morgan (170w)
"The fresh fruits that surround and tempt the child may be unfamiliar to American readers. Many are typical of the Caribbean, and they are referred to here by their Jamaican names—naseberry, sweetsop, pawpaw. Most will intrigue readers, even the guinep, about which the narrator explains: 'It don't mek no sense to pick it/ One guinep can't feed a cricket.' Axtell's rich, vibrant illustrations capture Jamaican life as decidedly as the orally based text that utilizes island patois to capture local speech patterns. Children will relish the little girl's sense of humor and her ability to outwit adults, and even the grand, grand stomach she has at the end. An unusual counting book with an engaging protagonist and an appealing look at rural Jamaican life."

REVIEW: Bull Cent Child Books v50 p275 Ap '97. Elizabeth Bush (180w)
"Counting is really just a happy excuse for Bloom's juicy verse. . . . Even without the benefit of illustration, the narrator's joyful cunning and sly wit suffuse the verse. Axtell's grainy full-page scenes, in a palette of tropical fruit colors that manage to be brilliant but not garish, are a glorious bonus, and the opening glossary of exotic fruits will set the taste buds tingling. Adult readers who are timid about tackling the island Patwa should just throw caution to the wind; it would be a shame to leave this one hanging on the vine."

BLOOM & BLOSSOM; the reader's guide to gardening; edited by Mary Swander. 275p $25 1997 Ecco Press
   810.8   1. Gardens—Literary collections 2. Gardening—Literary collections
   ISBN 0-88001-473-3   LC 96-26828

SUMMARY: This is a collection of writings about gardens and gardening. "The four sections each have a theme: the connection between garden and family, seeds, the garden in the natural world, and the garden in history and society." (Libr J)

REVIEW: Booklist v93 p1214 Mr 15 '97. Alice Joyce (130w)
"Swander's compilation contains a few historical excerpts together with nourishing, heaping helpings of contemporary thought culled from an abundance of recent garden literature. Many highly respected writers that have already won the hearts and minds of garden lovers are included—Michael Pollan, Eleanor Perenyi, Roger Swain, and Alan Lacy, among others. With poems sprinkled throughout, the essays and passages touch on topics both poignant and serious, such as the state of farming today and various views on our interdependence with the natural world."

what the purpose of the book is and many include acknowledgments (thanks to certain people for providing permissions, being of help, etc.). Further, many books include an introduction that frequently includes instructions on using the book. This is particularly true of books with many charts and tables. The introduction also may provide background information that makes the text easier to understand or use. The introduction is not necessarily written by the author. Students too frequently ignore a book's introduction, which leads sometimes to confusion in interpreting or using information it provides.

The text is the main body of the work. The appendixes (often spelled "appendices") might include a bibliography, index, maps, charts, graphs, etc., which have been added after the text. Consulting the bibliography will lead to additional sources of information. Using the index will help find information in the text easily and quickly. Some books may have a detailed table of contents in the front of the book that supplements or replaces the index. Most books have some sort of table of contents for locating general categories.

Book Review Sources

Book Review Digest, 1905– . New York: H. W. Wilson, 1905– .
Book Review Index, 1965– . Detroit: Gale Research, 1965– .
Book Review Index to Social Science Periodicals. Ann Arbor, MI: Pierian Press, 1978– (contents begin with 1964).
Current Book Review Citation, 1976–1982. New York: H. W. Wilson, 1976–1982.
Index to Book Reviews in the Humanities, 1960– . Detroit: Phillip, Thompson, 1960– .

Exercises for Chapter 6

1. Look carefully at the title page, back of the title page, table of contents, and index of this book. Note how they are arranged and what information is included.
2. Select one of the books about Princess Diana that you found in BIP or CBI (Chapter 5) and look for reviews in the book review sources in your library.

Important Terms in Chapter 6

anthologies   Choice
ISBN   *digest*
New York Times Index

7. General Information Sources

Objectives

After studying this chapter the student shall be able to
  • distinguish among the various types of dictionaries and determine
    which is appropriate for a particular word
  • use a variety of encyclopedias to research a topic
  • list the subject dictionaries and encyclopedias in a particular sub-
    ject field
  • list the handbooks, yearbooks and directories available in a par-
    ticular field and obtain information available from them
  • look up specific information in almanacs and other sources
  • find and use gazetteers and atlases

Occasionally students seek answers to specific questions or definitions for particular words. The resources that supply these answers are
called *general information sources*. Students have probably used some or
all references previously in school, although they didn't know how to
use them efficiently. The following discussion concerns the more common sources of general information and some alternate sources.

General Dictionaries

The most commonly used reference book is the dictionary. Yet
students are often unaware that there are different types of dictionaries
devised for particular uses. For most purposes a standard abridged desk

size dictionary such as The *American Heritage Dictionary* is satisfactory for finding definitions of words, spelling and pronunciation. However, the standard dictionary is abridged, that means that the editors have selected the more commonly used words in the language and omitted many that are uncommon. If the student cannot locate a particular word in the standard dictionary he should consult an unabridged dictionary such as *Webster's Third New International Dictionary of the English Language Unabridged*. This volume contains many of, but not all, the words in the language, including the archaic (out of date) words, slang words an acronyms (words formed by accumulating the first letters of each of several words). These volumes are huge and expensive and are thus unlikely to be found outside of the library. These dictionaries may include special sections in the back that may be useful. A gazetteer is an alphabetical listing of famous or not-so-famous place names. Some sections contain short biographies of famous persons, such as royalty or presidents of the United States. Others contain specialized information such as flags of the countries of the world, population counts and dates of important events. A brief perusal of the back of the dictionary takes only a minute or two, but will save time later. Before using any dictionary the student should consult the directions found in the front of the book to understand the format of definitions and special symbols used, particularly pronunciation symbols.

Special Dictionaries

Although consulting an abridged or unabridged dictionary may provide all the information that is necessary, other special dictionaries may be checked for additional or more specific information. Some of these specialized volumes are dictionaries of slang, abbreviations, rhyming (containing lists of words that rhyme, especially useful when writing poetry), synonyms (words with the same or similar meanings), antonyms (words that have opposite meaning) and acronyms.

Using dictionaries such as *A Dictionary of Modern English Usage* by Henry Fowler is an essential tool in writing. This dictionary deals with points of grammar, syntax, style, and proper use of words and their spelling and preferred pronunciation and punctuation. It also contains commonly used foreign words and their meanings. There is even a dictionary containing commonly mispronounced words and another with commonly misspelled words. There are many foreign language dictionaries translating words from one language to another as well as dictionaries of archaic languages such as Joseph T. Shipley's *Dictionary of Early English*. A thesaurus is a kind of dictionary that lists synonyms and related words for each entry word. A thesaurus is useful when you know the definition of a word and want another way of expressing it.

Subject Dictionaries

Dictionaries have been compiled for special subject fields. Often the meaning of words vary when they are found in different subject contexts. For example, the word "mutant" in general usage usually refers to some product of genetic failure; however, the biological meaning of mutant is "any abrupt change in genetic structure," good or bad. These subject dictionaries clarify such subtle differences in meaning. The subject dictionary is considered a secondary source when the standard dictionary does not provide subtle differences.

The definitions supplied in subject dictionaries are devised by experts in that field and may differ from field to field. Subject dictionaries provide a more detailed and specific contextual definition and may provide cross-references to other useful terms. To locate these special dictionaries the subject headings in the catalog should be used. The same rules for subject headings stated in Chapter 4 apply to subject dictionaries. Also the librarian may guide one to the proper heading.

Encyclopedias

Encyclopedias, like dictionaries, come in a variety of types. The most familiar type is the multi-volume general encyclopedia, such as the *Americana*, *Britannica* or *World Book*. Encyclopedias are also available on CDs. These may be available at the school library or purchased for use at home with your personal computer. There are also multi-volume encyclopedias in foreign languages, such as *Encyclopedia Universalis* (French), and *Gran Enciclopedia Rialp* (Spanish). Subject encyclopedias in both single volume and multi-volume sets are available. These subject encyclopedias are a valuable source of specific information. They include more detailed explanations than the ones given in general encyclopedias.

Examples of subject encyclopedias found in libraries are: *The Encyclopedia of Philosophy, The Catholic Encyclopedia, International Encyclopedia of the Social Sciences, Grove's Dictionary of Music and Musicians, Encyclopedia of World Art* and *McGraw-Hill Encyclopedia of Science and Technology.* These are just a few examples of the hundreds of subject encyclopedias available. Most topical areas have encyclopedias associated with them.

The information in encyclopedias is updated, but not necessarily regularly. Information is added and deleted with new editions. The size of the article may change with new editions depending on new information and space available. Some articles go unchanged for ten years or longer. One must read the introductory statement in an encyclopedia to determine its policy on updating information and its frequency of publishing new editions. Some encyclopedias contain a manual to help in using that particular set. Finally, encyclopedias contain only summaries of important information and should not be considered the final word. One should keep in mind also that articles are usually written by individual experts and may contain opinions with which not every expert agrees.

Handbooks, Directories...

Everyone, at one time or another, needs some bit of information and thinks, "There must be a quick way to find this." There are many reference books that provide specific short answers and facts. Handbooks instruct on how to find and use this information. Handbooks are available on all subjects. It is vital to become familiar with the ones in a major field of interest and students may even wish to purchase one in their chosen field. *The Library Research Guide to Nursing* by Strauch contains information on the use of reference books and the major ones available, lists of indexes and available periodicals published in nursing. *The Handbook of Chemistry* contains graphs, tables and charts that are used frequently.

Yearbooks contain updated information in particular subject fields. These are extremely valuable, because besides periodicals, they contain the most current information available. *The Annual Review of Psychology* has summaries of selected topics with extensive bibliographies. These topics, however, vary from year to year. Such reviews are excellent starting points for researching topics for a paper since they are current and complete. A student or practitioner in a particular field would be well-advised to purchase or periodically read the annual reviews.

Almanacs are particularly handy in that they provide some unusually specific or obscure information. The *World Almanac* contains data such as the capitals of all the countries of the world, weights and measures used,

Most libraries have a collection of phone books for the local area and major metropolitan centers.

the birth and death dates of famous persons, zip codes, addresses, population figures, records, and maps and so on. It is also an inexpensive purchase. Besides a dictionary, the almanac is a wise acquisition for the student. Although data are added or changed yearly, an almanac several years old is still valuable. Most libraries own several almanacs, which increases the probability that a particular item of information may be found.

Directories cover many subjects. Of course, the telephone book is a directory. Basically, all directories are lists of names, addresses and phone numbers. Some directories are annotated; that is, they include some explanation about the organization or corporation listed. See the list after this chapter for examples of directories. Information that may not appear in almanacs and encyclopedias may be found in statistical yearbooks and newspaper and periodical indexes.

If current events information is needed and the newspapers are unable to supply the needed information, try another current source such as *Keesing's Contemporary Archives, Congressional Quarterly Weekly Report* or *Facts on File*. Most libraries will have at least one of these sources. The Internet also provides current information and in some sites information is updated as often as minutely (stock market quotes, for example).

Atlases and Gazetteers

There are many sources providing geographical information. Encyclopedias, almanacs and telephone directories all provide some geographical information and maps. Further, travel guides are valuable sources of information, including maps and textual information. Some travel guides are commercially produced hardcover books and others are inexpensive paperbacks produced by organizations such as the big oil companies (Mobil and Exxon travel guides, for example). Some organizations such as the American Automobile Association (AAA) also produce comprehensive travel guides. Commercially produced guides, of course, may be somewhat biased.

Commonly used sources of geographical information are atlases and gazeteers. Atlases contain maps and charts with all sorts of geographical information. Consult the map of the library you produced in Chapter 1 to locate atlases in the library. Besides a collection of maps, they frequently contain: 1. Population data; 2. Mileage charts; 3. Statistics on imports and exports; 4. Information on rainfall, agricultural and natural resources; 5. Tourist attractions and national parks; and 6. Photographs of cities and scenery. Gazetteers are lists of place names and people. A gazetteer is very helpful in locating places which have undergone a name change. Gazetteers may be separate volumes or appended to atlases.

Exercises for Chapter 7

1. Look up and record (briefly) the meaning of "memory" in the following:
   an unabridged dictionary
   an abridged dictionary
   any biological dictionary
   any social sciences dictionary
   any thesaurus

2. Look up and record the meaning(s) of "hip" in the following:
an unabridged dictionary
an abridged dictionary
any slang dictionary
any abbreviations dictionary
any acronyms dictionary

3. (A) Look up your home state or your hometown in two different encyclopedias (e.g., Americana and World Book and compare the entries.

   (B) Look up "organic gardening" in two general encyclopedias and any subject encyclopedia you think may include an entry. Compare the articles and indicate the titles of the encyclopedias you checked.

4. List the subject dictionaries and encyclopedias in your major field of interest. Record the call numbers for future reference.

5. Locate on the shelves all the titles listed in question 4. Indicate which items circulate and which ones are multi-volume sets.

6. Take a term or concept in your major field of interest and look it up in a general encyclopedia and an encyclopedia in that subject. List the term or concept and briefly compare the articles.

7. Using the catalog, make a list of handbooks and guides in your library that deal with your major field of interest.

8. Locate in the catalog and on the shelves the almanacs and telephone directories. Do they circulate? If yes, explain briefly.

9. In general do yearbooks like *Statistical Abstracts of the United States* and the ones published by the United Nations circulate? Explain why or why not.

10. Using almanacs and statistical sources, look up your hometown or state and the college you attend (or one you know about).

    (A) How does this information on your hometown compare to what you found in the encyclopedia earlier?

    (B) Is the information about the college accurate?

    (C) Where else might you look for information about colleges?

11. (A) What kind of information does the telephone directory provide in the yellow pages? The Blue Pages?

    (B) Are zip codes in the phone book? If yes, where?

    (C) Are area codes listed in the phone book? If so, where?

    (D) What information about a community can be obtained by looking through the yellow pages, green pages, blue pages, and other sections?

12. Using the types of sources discussed in this chapter, answer the following questions. List the sources checked and those which provided information useful in answering the question.
   (A) Using three sources, find the address, zip code and phone number of McGraw-Hill, Inc., publishers.
   (B) Using at least three sources, find the population of Chicago, Illinois.
   (C) Using five sources, list the population, geographical area and political leaders of Canada.
13. Check the catalog and record the titles and call numbers of two gazetteers in your library.
14. Locate the atlases in your library, look through five, and record the types of information they contain in addition to maps.

Important Terms for Chapter 7

almanacs	*directory*
handbooks	*atlas*
yearbooks	*gazetteer*
unabridged	*synonyms*
abridged	*antonyms*
thesaurus	*acronyms*

Important Books for Chapter 7

DIRECTORIES

American Art Directory, v. 1– , 1898– . New York: Bowker, 1899– . Every 3 years, 1952– . Addresses and information about art organizations, and traveling booking agencies.

Annual Directory of Environmental Information Sources, 1971– . Boston: National Foundation for Environmental Control, 1971– . Addresses of agencies and organizations, lists of books, documents, reports, periodicals and films on the environment.

Darney, Bridgitte T., and Janice DeMaggio. *Subject Directory of Special Libraries*. 13th ed. Detroit: Gale Research Corp., 1989. (3 vols.)

Encyclopedia of Associations. Detroit: Gale Research, 1956– . Revised approximately every 2 years; 4 vol. Addresses and descriptions of organizations. Also lists defunct organizations.

National Faculty Directory, 1970– . Detroit: Gale Research, 1970– . Annual, 3 vols. Names and college or university affiliations of full-time teaching faculty. Schools not listed did not submit requested information.

New York State Industrial Directory, 1959– . New York: State Industrial Directories Corp., 1959– . Annual, Available for each of the 50 states. Names and addresses of industries including company offices, number of employees and products manufactured.

Newby, Gregory B. *Directory of Directories on the Internet: A Guide to Information Sources.* Westport, Ct.: Meckler Media, 1994.

Towell, Julie, and Charles B. Montney. *Directories in Print.* Detroit: Gale Research 1989– . Annual. (Formerly *The Directory of Directories.*) An annotated classified list of directories with title and subject index.

ALMANACS

Barone, Michael. *Almanac of American Politics.* Washington, D.C.: National Journal, 1972– . Annual. Arranged by state. Includes state and congressional districts, elected officials, campaign financing, congressional committees, etc.

Catholic Almanac. Huntington, IN: Our Sunday Visitor, Inc., 1969–. Annual. Catholic church organization, doctrine, history and brief descriptions of other religions, some statistics.

Information Please Almanac, Atlas and Yearbook, 1947– . Planned and supervised by Dan Golenpaul Associates. New York: Simon & Schuster, 1947– . Annual. Miscellaneous information, extensive historical and statistical information on the U.S., a general subject index and short biography section.

Japan Almanac. Tokyo: Mainichi Newspapers. In English, short articles on many aspects of Japanese history, culture and daily life, statistics and biographies, index.

The World Almanac and Book of Facts, 1868– . New York: World Telegram, 1868– . Annual. Now published by Pharos Books and distributed by St. Martin's Press. Up-to-date, reliable statistics; most comprehensive and most frequently used of all U.S. almanacs.

ENCYCLOPEDIAS

The Catholic Encyclopedia: An International Work of References on the Constitution, Doctrine, Discipline and History of the Catholic Church.

New York: Catholic Encyclopedia Press, 1907–1922. 17 vols. Many long articles by experts. In addition to Catholic doctrine articles on general subjects such as literature and history. Somewhat out of date but still valuable. For newer information see the *New Catholic Encyclopedia* published by McGraw-Hill, 1967.

Encyclopedia of Bioethics. Warren T. Reich, ed. Rev. Simon & Schuster Macmillan, 1995, 5 vols. Deals with many aspects of bioethics including such questions as abortion, euthanasia and the definition of death.

Encyclopedia of Ethics. Lawrence C. Becker, ed. New York: Garland, 1992. 2 vols.

Encyclopedia of Psychology. Raymond J. Corsini, ed. 2nd ed. New York: John Wiley & Sons, 1994. 4 vols. Contains biographies and short articles on theories, research and concepts in psychology.

Encyclopedia of Sociology. Edgar F. Borgatta, editor in chief. New York: Macmillan, 1992. 4 vols. Part of the update to the *International Encyclopedia of the Social Sciences.*

Encyclopedia of World Art. New York: McGraw-Hill, 1959–1968. Fifteen vols. plus two supplementary vols. Long articles with bibliographies. Approximately half of each volume is plates. All areas of art are included as well as all countries and periods.

International Encyclopedia of the Social Sciences. David L. Sill, ed. New York: Macmillan and the Free Press, 1968. 18 vols. Articles deal with all aspects of the social sciences, many cross references are included, some biographies and a good index. Updates have been issued as encyclopedias in various areas such as criminal law, justice, Third World, etc. Most of these are 2–4 volumes.

McGraw-Hill Encyclopedia of Science and Technology. An international reference work, 8th ed.. New York: McGraw-Hill, 1997. 20 vols. Covers all branches of science except medicine and the behavioral sciences. Index volume. The set is kept updated with annual yearbooks.

Worldmark Encyclopedia of the Nations, 7th ed. Moshe Y. Sachs, ed. New York: John Wiley, 1988; distributed by Worldmark Press. 5 vols. Volume 1 is for U.N.; other volumes for Africa, Americas, Europe and Asia and Oceania.

YEARBOOKS

Demographic Yearbook/Annuaire Demographique, 1948– . New York: United Nations, 1948– . International demographic statistics from approximately 220 countries. This is one of a series of statistical yearbooks compiled by the United Nations.

Historic Documents of 19XX– . Washington, DC: Congressional Quarterly, Inc., 1972– . Annual. Chronological arrangement of speeches, letters, reports, etc., of importance. Cumulative index included in each volume. Detailed table of contents.

Statesman's Yearbook: A Statistical and Historical Account of the States of the World, 1864– . London, New York: Macmillan, 1864–. Not an almanac but brief and reliable descriptions, statistical information about countries of the world. Includes the countries' leaders, ambassadors and embassies and a bibliography of statistical information for each country.

United Nations. Statistical Office. *Yearbook of International Trade Statistics, 1950–* . New York: United Nations, 1951– . Annual. Provides annual trade statistics, imports and exports, many tables have comparative figures for several years.

United States Bureau of the Census. *Statistical Abstracts of the United States, 1878–* . Washington, D.C.: U.S. Gov. Printing Office, 1879– . Annual. Statistical summaries, most tables cover several years. First source to use national statistics. Leads users to other important statistical sources. Has useful supplements such as *County and City Data Book.*

HANDBOOKS AND GUIDES

Altman, Philip, and Dorothy S. Dittmer, eds. *Biology Data Book*, 2nd ed. Bethesda, MD: Federation of American Societies of Experimental Biology, 1972–1974. 3 vols. Tabular data for life sciences, includes some descriptive data. Each volume has a separate index.

Frick, Elizabeth. *History: Illustrated Search Strategy and Sources.* 2nd ed. Ann Arbor, MI: Pierian Press, 1995. This is the latest in a series of library research guides from Pierian Press. They include information on selecting topics, organizing term papers, using the literature in the field (includes sample pages of reference sources), computerized literature searching an other aspects of library research.

Gibaldi, Joseph, and Walter S. Achtert. *MLA Handbook for Writers of Research Papers*, 4th ed. New York: Modern Language Association of America, 1995. Widely used standards for preparation of articles, papers and books. This style information is also found in several term paper guides. See the bibliography at the end of Chapter 16.

Handbook of Chemistry and Physics. A ready reference book of chemical and physical data. Cleveland: Chemical Rubber, 1913– . 71st ed., 1990–1991.

Mullins, Carolyn J. *A Guide to Writing and Publishing in the Social Sciences.* New York: John Wiley, 1977. Guide to and information about writing papers, reports and articles for publication in the social sciences.

South American Handbook. A yearbook and guide to the countries and resources of South and Central America, Mexico and the West Indies, 1924– . London: Trade and Travel Pubs., 1924– . Descriptions of national history, government, travel and other information on the countries included.

SPECIAL DICTIONARIES

Aitchison, Jean. *International Thesaurus of Refugee Terminology.* Boston: M. Nijhoff, 1989.

Allen, Frederick Sturges. *Allen's Synonyms and Antonyms.* Rev. ed. Edited by T. H. Vail Motter. New York: Harper, 1938.

Bender, James Frederick. *NBC Handbook of Pronunciation*, 3rd ed., rev. by Thomas Lee Crowell, Jr. New York: Crowell, 1964.

Butress, F. A. *World Guide to Abbreviations of Organizations*, 8th ed., Detroit: Gale Research, 1987.

DeSola, Ralph. *Abbreviations Dictionary*, 6th ed. New York: Elsevier, 1981.

Fowler, Henry Watson. *Dictionary of Modern English Usage.* 2nd rev. ed. Edited by Sir Ernst Gowers. Oxford, England: Clarendon Press, 1965. Reprinted 1987.

Johnson, Burgess. *New Rhyming Dictionary and Poet's Handbook.* Rev. ed. New York: Harper, 1957.

Major, Clarence. *Dictionary of Afro-American Slang.* New York: International, 1970.

Oxford Dictionary of English Etymology, ed. by C. T. Onions with the assistance of C. W. S. Friedrichsen and R. W. Burchfield. Oxford, England: Clarendon Press, 1966.

Oxford English Dictionary, 2nd ed. Edited by J. A. Simpson and Edmund S. Weiner. Oxford, England: Oxford University Press, 1989. 20 vols.

Random House Historical Dictionary of American Slang. J. E. Lighter, ed. New York: Random House, 1994.

Roget's International Thesaurus, 5th ed. Edited by Robert L. Chapman. New York: HarperCollins, 1992. New York: Crowell, 1977.

Shaw, Henry. *Punctuate It Right!* 2nd ed. New York: Harper Perennial, 1993.

ATLASES AND GAZETTEERS

Alexander, Gerald L. *Guide to Atlases: World, Regional, National, Thematic.* Metuchen, NJ: Scarecrow, 1971. An international listing of atlases published since 1950.

American Geographical Society of New York. Maps Department. *Index to Maps in Books and Periodicals.* Boston: G. K. Hall, 1969. 10 vols., supplements in 1971, 1976, 1987.

Barraclough, Geoffrey, ed. *The Times Atlas of World History*, 3rd rev. ed. Maplewood, NJ: Hammond, 1989.

Chambers World Gazetteer: A Geographical Dictionary. Edited by David Munro. New York: Cambridge University Press, 1990. Reprint of a 1988 edition with a slightly different title.

Cobb, David A. *Guide to U.S. Map Resources.* 2nd ed. Chicago: American Library Association, 1990.

Columbia Lippincott Gazetteer of the World. Ed. by Leon E. Seltzer with the Geographical Research Staff of Columbia University Press and with the cooperation of the American Geographical Society, with 1961 suppl. New York: Columbia University Press, 1962.

George Philip & Son. *Oxford Atlas of the World.* 4th ed. New York: Oxford University Press, 1996.

Goode's World Atlas. Edward B. Espenshade, Jr., Senior editor, Consultant Joel L. Morrison. 18th ed. Chicago: Rand McNally, 1990.

Kopal, Zdenek. *A New Photographic Atlas of the Moon.* New York: Taplinger, 1971.

NBC News Rand McNally World News Atlas, 1991. New York: Rand McNally, 1990. Published anually. Covers selected world events of the previous year.

Nelson, Theodora. *Good Books for the Curious Traveler: Europe.* Boulder, CO: Johnson Books, 1989.

Oxford Economic Atlas of the World. Prep. by the Cartographic Dept. of Clarendon Press, 4th ed. London: Oxford University Press, 1972.

Rand McNally and Company. *Rand McNally Premier World Atlas.* Chicago: Rand McNally, 1997.

Rand McNally and Co. *Rand McNally World Atlas*. Census ed. Chicago: Rand McNally, 1992.

Rand McNally Concise World Atlas. New York: Rand McNally, 1987.

Shepherd, William Robert. *Historical Atlas*. 9th ed. New York: Barnes & Noble, 1964. Reprinted 1980.

Special Libraries Association. Geography and Map Division. Directory Revision Committee. *Map Collections in the United States and Canada: A Directory*, 4th ed. New York: Special Libraries Association, 1985.

The Times. London. *The Times Atlas of the World: Comprehensive Edition*. 8th ed. London: Times Books, 1990. Considered the best atlas available.

U.S. Board on Geographical Names. *Gazetteer*, no. 130–142. Washington, D.C. GOP, 1974–1977.

Webster's New Geographical Dictionary. Rev. ed. Springfield, MA: G. & C. Merriam, 1984.

Wright, George Ernest, and Floyd Vivian Filson. *The Westminster Historical Atlas to the Bible*. Rev. ed. Philadelphia: Westminster, 1956.

8. Periodicals and Newspapers

Objectives

After studying this chapter the student shall be able to
- identify the different types of periodicals and locate them in the library
- find specific information in periodicals
- distinguish between indexes and abstracts
- locate appropriate indexes and abstracts and use them to find information
- determine how to find periodicals at remote libraries
- find specific information in newspapers

Periodical Indexes

What is a periodical? What is a journal? What is a magazine? Students and teachers frequently use these terms. While there are slight differences in their meanings, for the purposes of this discussion these terms are identical and will be used interchangeably. They are publications that appear at regular, short intervals and contain articles, stories, poems, and essays about a specific subject, aimed at a specific age group, or at some other grouping determined by the editors.

For some students, the use of periodicals can be frustrating. They can't find anything pertinent in them. This is unfortunate because periodicals are vital in preparing most reports or term papers. The information in them is usually more current than the information in books.

Figure 8.1 General Science Index

Water intake *See* Drinking (Physiology)
Water laws and regulations
　　See also
　　Clean Water Act
Bond Act benefits New York's fish and wildlife resources. il
　N Y State Conservationist v51 p supp 2 Je '97
EPA prepares for state nonpoint source controls. *Environ Sci
　Technol* v31 p306A-307A Jl '97
Watershed management approach gains with states. J. Pelley.
　il *Environ Sci Technol* v31 p322A-323A Jl '97
Water level
　　See also
　　Sea level
Water pollution
　　See also
　　Estuarine pollution
　　Groundwater pollution
　　Groundwater remediation technologies
　　Marine pollution
　　Oil pollution of rivers, harbors, etc.
　　Radioactive substances in the water
　　Water—Microbiology
　　Water as carrier of infection
　　　　Detection and monitoring
Arsenic and old waste [H. E. Hemond studies arsenic contami-
　nation of lakes and sediment] K. S. Brown. por *MIT
　Technol Rev* v100 p10 My/Je '97
Experimental investigations of water quality: the bioassay. J. E.
　Havel and others. bibl *Am Biol Teach* v59 p349-52 Je '97
First U.S. contaminated sediments report released. *Environ Sci
　Technol* v31 p306A Jl '97
Use of CUSUM methods for water-quality monitoring in stor-
　ages. R. M. Nally and B. T. Hart. bibl *Environ Sci
　Technol* v31 p2114-19 Jl '97
The use of enterococcus and coliform in characterizing bath-
　ing-beach waters. R. Nuzzi and R. Burhans. bibl il map *J
　Environ Health* v60 p16-22 Jl/Ag '97
　　　　Indicator organisms

Influence of various filters on the concentration of pesticides
　dissolved in water. C. Mouvet and C. Jücker. bibl il *Environ
　Sci Technol* v31 p2434-7 Ag '97
Water resources *See* Water supply
Water rights *See* Water laws and regulations
Water softening
Sodium content of well water vs. local municipal water. B.
　Apgar. *Am Fam Phys* v56 p580+ Ag '97
Water sports *See* Aquatic sports
Water supply
　　See also
　　Reservoirs
　　Watersheds
Water resources: agriculture, the environment, and society. D.
　Pimentel and others. bibl il *BioScience* v47 p97-106 F '97;
　Discussion. v47 p402 Jl/Ag '97
Water table *See* Groundwater
Water temperature
　　See also
　　Ocean temperature
Water vapor
　　See also
　　Humidity
External supply of oxygen to the atmospheres of the giant
　planets. H. Feuchtgruber and others. bibl il *Nature* v389
　p159-62 S 11 '97
Pipelines to the planets. D. M. Hunten. bibl il *Nature* v389
　p125-6 S 11 '97
Water waves
　　See also
　　Ocean waves
　　Tidal waves
Watercraft, Personal *See* Jet skis
Watersheds
PHS in the Queen City: a watershed development [PHS chron-
　icles] L. P. Snyder. il *Public Health Rep* v112 p347-50
　Jl/Ag '97

Finding information in periodicals is not hopeless if the student uses the indexes to periodicals as tools.

Everyone has used an index of some sort, and most people are familiar with the indexes at the back of books. Everyone has used the yellow pages of a telephone directory, which is a type of index.

Individual periodicals may include an index for each volume or multi-volume indexes. Yet, these indexes are useful only if one knows which volume is needed. Unfortunately, this is not the typical situation. Therefore, *subject* indexes are more useful than *volume* indexes.

If students need the titles of journals published in a specific subject, they should consult a periodical directory. They are usually arranged by subject or have a subject index. Libraries will have at least one of the following directories: *Magazines for Libraries, The Standard Periodical Directory* or *Ulrich's International Periodical Directory*. Directories of periodicals in broad subjects (e.g. science) are also available. To enable one to find information published in journals, many comprehensive indexes and abstracts are available and are grouped into four categories:

1. *general*, that includes all relevant journals
2. *subject*, that are topic specific
3. *current*, only those of the present year or past two years
4. *retrospective*, covering a specific period of years.

The most recent issues of periodicals are displayed for easy access.

Many are published by the same company and are in the same format. Having learned to use the "Wilson index" format, one can use almost every other index. The major difference between indexes is in which periodicals are included. The formats are similar.

An entry in a Wilson index under a particular subject heading includes:

1. title of the article
2. author's name
3. title of the journal, frequently abbreviated
4. date, which may include day, month and year
5. volume number
6. issue number
7. pages (see Figure 8.1)

Various indexes may not provide the information in the same order but all the information will be included. Indexes are published weekly, biweekly, monthly, quarterly and semiannually.

Perhaps the best known index and the most used is the *Reader's Guide to Periodical Literature* (RGPL), H. W. Wilson, publisher. The *Reader's Guide* indexes approximately 220 periodicals of general interest (popular magazines) and contains magazines such as *Life, Sports*

Figure 8.2 General Science Index
(OCLC FirstSearch Screen)

You searched for the WORD: experimental investigations water quality

Record #1 of 1

AUTHOR   Havel, John E.

TITLE   Experimental investigations of water quality: the
     bioassay.

IMPRINT   United States 1997

DESC.   p. 349-52 : bibl.

NOTE   Bioassays that can be used in classroom investigations
     of water quality are described. In these bioassays, the
     responses of aquatic species to NaCl are measured. The
     effect of salt concentration on the survival of the 2
     cladocerans Ceriodaphnia dubia and Daphnia sp. was
     measured, and the concentration of salt resulting in the
     death of half of the population, or the 50 percent
     lethal concentration, was determined. The effect of
     salt concentration on behavior and fertility was also
     examined, and the 50 percent inhibitory concentration
     was obtained.

SUBJECT   Biological assay.

Water Analysis.

     Water pollution Detection and monitoring.

ADD AUTHOR Barnhart, M. Christopher. Greene, Janice Schnake.

APPEARS IN nnas The American Biology Teacher v. 59 (June '97) p.
     349-52 Am Biol Teach 0002-7685

OCLC CODES LIBRARIES: STATE: NY LIBRARY: BNG BUF COO CTX NAB NAK
     NAM NYA NYB NYG NYS RRR RVA RVE SDE SGD SHB SYB VDM VDN
     VFI VFL VFQ VGA VGF VGK VHB VJA VJK VJN VKC VKQ VKY VMY
     VMZ VNB VOC VOQ VOX VQT VSI VVC VVH VVN VVX VWB VXE VXG
     VXI VXO VXV VXW VXX VXZ VYA VYF VYL VYS VZE VZF VZG VZJ
     VZK VZN VZU VZV VZX WUC WUJ XAA XAF XAN XBM XFM XFV XIM
     XJM XLM XMA XME XNC XQM XSC XTA YAH YAM YBM YCM YDD YFF
     YFM YGB YGD YGM YHM YJA YJJ YJT YKC YKE YKJ YKN YKU YLC
     YOM YPM YPW YSM YTM YYP ZBM ZDG ZEM ZHC ZHM ZIH ZLI ZLM
     ZNT ZOW ZQC ZQM ZQP ZSJ ZWC ZWU ZXC

Illustrated, *Time* and *U.S. News*. The *Readers Guide* is current and general. An example of a general, retrospective index is *Poole's Index to Periodical Literature* that covers the years 1802–1906. An example of a current and subject index is the *Business Periodicals Index*, which indexes approximately 300 journals in the fields of business and economics.

FirstSearch

OCLC's FirstSearch is available from more than 10,600 libraries worldwide. New FirstSearch introduced in 1999 includes 75 databases/

Most libraries keep a 3-month backfile of newspapers.

indexes covering the fields of humanities, sciences and social studies. Individual libraries contract with OCLC to make some or all of First-Search databases available. FirstSearch may be an option on the OPAC or accessed via a terminal devoted to the Internet.

Many Wilson indexes are available on FirstSearch. Figure 8.2 is an entry from *General Science Index.* Compare it's format and information with the same entry in Figure 8.1 (print copy of *General Science Index).* Note that the entry contains the same information PLUS a long note; assigned subject headings and the OCLC libraries in New York State that hold the journal in which the article appears. The search in Figure 8.2 was done via an INNOPAC catalog in New York State that uses Z39.50. If a holdings list is included in the entry it's scope is determined by the library where the search is conducted. Not all libraries use the same Internet access to FirstSearch and entries may appear different. See Figures 8.4 and 8.5 to compare formats for the same entry from PsychFirst.

CARL

The CARL Corporation Network and Uncover is based in Colorado. As of March 1998 CARL offered access to over 20 commercial databases and more than 420 library catalogs. The Uncover databases; UNCOVER EXPRESS, and some of the other commercial databases allow access by any user. Other databases require licensing and the use of a password or a library card. The CARL System Library Catalogs are open to all users.

The welcome menu indicates which databases are open to all users with no required password. Among the free access databases are Uncover (periodical index and document delivery); open access databases and CARL System Library Catalogs. The open access databases include the British Library Document Supply Centre; U.S. Government Publication; CONSER (the serials records from the Library of Congress, part of New Serials Titles) and UNCOVER EXPRESS (articles available via FAX within I hour).

The Uncover indexing includes more than 4,000 current citations added daily. Uncover searching can be by *word* (which includes subject); *author* and *browse* (by journal title). The *word* search will find word(s) which appear in the title, subtitle, summary or abstract. The searcher may enter as many words as he likes as long as they all fit on one line. The search is conducted as if AND appears between each word. It might be best to start with just two or three words and see what results.

Figure 8.3 Psychological Abstracts

775. **Xerri, Christian; Stern, Judith M. & Merzenich, Michael M.** (U d'Aix-Marseille I, Faculté des Sciences de St Jérôme, Lab de Psychophysiologie, Marseille, France) **Alterations of the cortical representation of the rat ventrum induced by nursing behavior.** *Journal of Neuroscience,* 1994(Mar). Vol 14(3, Pt 2), 1710–1721. —Investigated neurological changes induced in 1 forebrain region, presumed to be involved in nursing behavior (NB). 13 adult female Long-Evans rats underwent mapping of trunk surfaces to assess cortical representational changes that might be induced in the somatosensory (SM) cortical field by a natural source of tactile inputs, i.e., stimulation of the rat ventrum in NB. Results indicate that the SM representation of the nipple-bearing skin of the anterior and posterior ventrum in these Ss expands about 2-fold in area for cortical maps derived 10–19 days after nursing onset. Receptive fields representing these differentially stimulated skin surfaces are reduced to approximately 33% of their control sizes. Thus, the regions of the ventrum skin surfaces surrounding the nipples that are most heavily stimulated in sucking come to be represented in finer topographic grain.

The system allows the searcher to narrow the search by adding an additional word. The search does not need to be retyped. When a specific entry is displayed it will include author; title; summary; where the article is located plus what it would cost to have a copy taxed. (See Figure 8.6). For more information CARL can be accessed via the Internet at uncover@carl.org or databases@carl.org.

Abstracts

Annotated indexes, known as abstracts, include additional information. They include all the information found in the index citation plus a brief description or summary of the article. This enables the user to figure out the content of the article without reading it. This may save time, enabling the user to select articles to be read in a quick and easy way. Yet, these abstracts may not always be accurate; caution is the watchword when using abstracts. If the student is unsure, it is advisable to consult the article directly before discarding it or quoting it. *Psychological Abstracts* (Figure 8.3) and *Chemical Abstracts* are annotated

Figure 8.4 OCLC Screen — PsychFirst

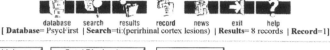

database   search   results   record   news   exit   help
[**Database**= PsychFirst | **Search**=ti:(perirhinal cortex lesions) | **Results**= 8 records | **Record**=1]

| Libraries with Item | | Get / Display Item | | E-Mail Record |

| ⬇ NextRec | ⬆ PrevRec |

Ownership: Check the catalogs in your library.

```
    RECORD NO: 84-34534
       AUTHOR: Falls, William A.; Bakken, Karl T.; Heldt, Scott A.
CORP. SOURCE: Northern Illinois U, Dept of Psychology, De Kalb, IL, US
        TITLE: Lesions of the perirhinal cortex interfere with conditioned
               excitation but not with conditioned inhibition of fear.
       SOURCE: Behavioral Neuroscience
         DATE: 1997 Jun Vol 111(3) 476-486
         YEAR: 1997
    ISSN/ISBN: 0735-7044
     LANGUAGE: English
    DOC. TYPE: Journal Article
     ABSTRACT: Posttraining lesions of the perirhinal cortex (Prh) have been
               shown to interfere with the expression of fear. This study
               assessed whether Prh lesions would also disrupt the inhibition
               of fear as measured with conditioned inhibition of fear-
               potentiated startle. Following light + shock, noise  light-no
               shock conditioned-inhibition training, rats were given Prh
               lesions. The lesions interfered with the expression of fear-
               potentiated startle to the light. To assess whether
               conditioned inhibition was affected, the rats were given light
               + retraining without additional noise  light - training. The
               noise-conditioned inhibitor retained its ability to inhibit
               fear-potentiated startle to the retrained light. These results
               suggest that the areas of the Prh that are essential for the
               initial expression of conditioned fear are not important for
               the expression of conditioned inhibition of fear. (PsycINFO
               Database Copyright 1997 American Psychological Assn, all
               rights reserved)
  MAJOR DESC: AMYGDALOID BODY; FEAR; STARTLE REFLEX
  MINOR DESC: BRAIN LESIONS; RATS
  KEY PHRASE: posttraining lesions of perirhinal cortex, inhibition of fear-
               potentiated startle to light & noise, male rats with lesions
               vs with sham lesions
 CLASS. CODE: 2520
```

| ⬇ NextRec | ⬆ PrevRec |

| Libraries with Item | | Get / Display Item | | E-Mail Record |

[TOP]   Databases   Search   Results   **Record**   News   Text Only   Exit   Help

FirstSearch
A world of information online

indexes. These are the most useful tools in writing papers and theses. Abstracts may be prepared by the author of the article or by someone else who probably works for the publisher or abstracting service. To find the title of indexes or abstracts in a specific field in the library, look under the subject (in the catalog) and then look for the subheading indexes or abstracts. For example, chemistry — abstracts — periodicals.

Indexes and abstracts are generally arranged by subject, although some indexes interfile authors with subjects in one alphabet. Others have separate author index and cross-references back to the subject section. The abstracts are usually numbered (see figures 8.3 and 8.4). Most abstracts begin each volume with number 1. It is important to consult the proper volume.

Some indexing/abstracting services also available in online or CD-ROM format also publish thesauruses of index terms. These thesauruses are as important to consult when searching the index or abstract as consulting LCSH when searching the catalog. The the-

Relax and catch up on the latest news.

saurus for *Psychological Abstracts/PsychINFO* is similar to LCSH in providing B for Broader terms, N for narrower terms, R for related terms, UF and USE, etc.

Some abstracts are also available via the Internet. For example, part of *Psychological Abstracts* is available from PsychFirst (found on First-Search). Compare Figure 8.3 (print edition), Figure 8.4 and 8.5 from PsychFirst. Figures 8.4 and 8.5 are the same entry from PsychFirst but located by searching from two different libraries. These libraries use different OPACs and programs to search FirstSearch. Note in Figure 8.4

Figure 8.5 OCLC Screen — PsychFirst (Innopac)

INNOPAC Z39.50 searching PsycFirst at FirstSearch Databases
You searched for the AUTHOR: falls william a
Record #3 of 7

AUTHOR   Falls, William A. Bakken, Karl T. Heldt, Scott A.

TITLE   Lesions of the perirhinal cortex interfere with conditioned
excitation but not with conditioned inhibition of fear.

IMPRINT   1997

SERIES   Northern Illinois U, Dept of Psychology, De Kalb, IL, US

NOTE   DOC. TYPE: Journal Article

     KEY PHRASE: posttraining lesions of perirhinal cortex, inhibition of fear-potentiated startle to light & noise, male rats with lesions vs with sham lesions

     CLASS. CODE: 2520

     Posttraining lesions of the perirhinal cortex (Prh) have been shown to interfere with the expression of fear. This study assessed whether Prh lesions would also disrupt the inhibition of fear as measured with conditioned inhibition of fear-potentiated startle. Following light + shock, noise light-no shock conditioned-inhibition training, rats were given Prh lesions. The lesions interfered with the expression of fear-potentiated startle to the light. To assess whether conditioned inhibition was affected, the rats were given light + retraining without additional noise light -training. The noise-conditioned inhibitor retained its ability to inhibit fear-potentiated startle to the retrained light. These results suggest that the areas of the Prh that are essential for the initial expression of conditioned fear are not important for the expression of conditioned inhibition of fear. (PsycINFO Database Copyright 1997 American Psychological Assn, all rights reserved)

SUBJECT   AMYGDALOID BODY FEAR STARTLE REFLEX
     BRAIN LESIONS RATS

APPEARS IN Behavioral Neuroscience 1997 Jun Vol 111(3) 476-486
     0735-7044

OCLC CODES LIBRARIES: STATE: NY LIBRARY: A8C BNG BUF
COO NAM NYB NYG RNM RRR RVA SBH SYB VDB VDH VFL VFQ
VFR VJA VKC VKM VQY VSI VVB VVC VVD VVL VVN VVO VVP
VVS VVU VVV VXF VXL VXO VXP VXW VXX VYE VYF VYL VYQ
VYS VZB VZE VZF VZH VZJ VZN VZP VZS VZU WJ7 XBM XFM XIB
XIM XLM XNC XQM XSC YAH YAM YBM YCJ YCM YFE YGM
YHM YOM YPI YPM YRM YSM YSW YTM YYE YYP ZBM ZCH ZCU
ZEM ZGM ZHM ZIH ZLI ZLM ZNT ZOW ZPM ZQM ZQP ZRS ZSJ
ZWC ZWU ZXC

that the *record number,* 84-34534 is the *Psychological Abstracts* number with 84 being the volume number and 34534 the abstract number. Note that in Figure 8.5 the search done on INNOPAC and using Z39.50 the information is the same EXCEPT the abstract or record number is excluded and the OCLC libraries holding the journal *Behavioral Neuroscience* are included.

Locating Journals

After the articles in the journals have been identified, the next step is to locate the journals in the library. Using the map constructed in Chapter 1 the location of the periodical stacks can be identified. These stacks usually contain the periodicals in alphabetical order. Each periodical may encompass several shelves. The indexes or abstracts provide the information needed about journal title, volume number, date and pages. The periodical's holdings list for the library is usually a circular or card file, list printed by OCLC, or available by searching the OPAC. This lists all the periodicals the library holds as well as the volumes owned. Journals for current months are usually located in a special section or reading area. Generally, periodicals do not circulate, since they are difficult or impossible to replace and are in high demand by library users.

Union List of Serials

What if the journal needed is not owned by the library? How can a library that owns the journal be identified? Union lists of serials show which libraries own which journals. They cover a range from local to international. The librarian may be consulted to locate the union lists. Libraries usually own the *Union List of Serials* (ULS), third edition (Figure 8.7) and its supplements, *New Serials Titles* (Figure 8.8). The codes used to identify the holding libraries are the same ones that are used in the *National Union Catalog*. Figure 8.9 from the Union List of Serials, third edition is from the periodical *Oregon Business Review*. The entry states that the journal is published in Oregon by the University of Oregon School of Business Administration, and that it began publication in December 1941. The two columns of letters represent the libraries that own this periodical. The number following each letter code shows the volume number of the beginning volume in the holdings. For this journal most of the libraries' holdings begin with volume 1. The (+) after the volume number shows that the libraries own all volumes after volume 1. A key to the codes is found at the beginning of each volume of the *Union List of Serials*. The *New Serials Titles* (NST) format was the same as NUC (see Figure 8.8). A brief look at the organization of the code will help to identify many libraries without having to consult the list. Generally the code has three letters, the first, the state, the second

Figure 8.6

AUTHOR(s): Dustin, Daniel L.
     Wolff, Robert M.
TITLE(s): Fifty Years of Stewardship: The Ongoing Struggle to Preserve Everglades National Park.
Summary: Everglades National Park, home to the largest continuous stand of sawgrass prairie in
North America, the predominant water recharge for south Florida, and the largest designated
wilderness habitat east of the Rocky Mountains, finds itself in an unenviable position. Problems
inside the park range from threatened flora and fauna to the maintenance of a steady supply of fresh
water.

     In: Parks & recreation.
          FEB 01 1998 v 33 n 2
        Page: 80
     SICI Code: 0031-2215(19980201)33:2L.80:FYSO;1-

This article may be available in your library, at no cost to you. To have
  it faxed from UnCover, the following charges apply:

Service Charge: $ 10.00
Fax Surcharge: $ .00
Copyright Fee: $ 3.00

Total Delivery Cost: 13.00

the city and the third the name of the university. Some codes are one or two letters and some four. For example, NNC: N is "New York," thus the first N is for New York State, the second N is for "New York City," and the C is for "Columbia University." Likewise NNU is for "New York University," N for "New York State," N for "New York City" and U for "University." If the second letter is lowercase it is part of the state; CtY, Ct is Connecticut and Y is "Yale." Journal articles needed by students or faculty may be borrowed from other libraries (see Chapter 14 for interlibrary loans).

Newspapers

Although printed information has been available for thousands of years, newspapers as we know them did not develop until the early 17th century. Before then proclamations were read aloud to large crowds and were posted in the village square. Other ways of transmitting news (besides the town crier and troubadours or ballad singers) included news pamphlets and newsletters. A news pamphlet is usually a short small sheet of paper, folded once to make four pages, and is concerned with one subject. A broadsheet refers to a single sheet of large size paper

Figure 8.7 Union List of Serials

commerce) Portland. v1-12 no3,S 10 1922-N
1931‖
    1,1922-Ag 1923 as Oregon journal of com-
    merce. v7 no8-v8 no7 omitted in number-
    ing
CSt   3-[8-11]   OrCA
CU   [4]-12   OrP   1-[10]
CtY   [4]-12   OrPR [3]-[8]
                           OrU   1[2]-[12]
IU   1-11
NN   1[2]-[12]   WaS   6-[11]12

**OREGON business and investors, inc., Port-
land, Ore.**
Bulletin. *See* Your taxes

OREGON business review. (Oregon. University.
*   School of business administration. Bureau
    of business research) Eugene. 1,D 24 1941+
AU   1+   MCM   1+
AzU   1+   MH-BA 1+
C   1+   MdBJ 1+
CLSU 1+
CSt   1+
CU   1+   N   1+
CoU   1+   NBuU 1+
Ct   1+   NIC   1+
CtY   1+   NN   1+
DL   1+   NNC   1+
FU   1+   NNU   1+
IEN   1+   NcD   1+
IU   1+   NmU   1+
IaU   1+   OCl   1+
IdU   1+   OOxM 1+
In   2+
InU   1+   OkU   1+
MBU   1+   OrCA 1+
OrP   1+   TxHR 4
OrPR 1+   UU   [1]+
OrU   1+   VU   1+
PPT   1+   WU   1+
PU   1+   WaS   1+
RKS   1+   WaU   1+
RPB   1+   WyU   1+

OREGON cancer control news. Portland. 1,N
    1916+
OrCA 2+   OrU-M 1+
OrP   1+   DNLM 1+

Figure 8.8   New Serial Titles

TITLE CHANGE
Equine business journal : EBJ. — Vol. 31, no. 10 (Oct.
   1990)-   — San Clemente, CA : Rich Publica-
   tions, 1990-
       v. : ill. ; 28 cm.
   Monthly.
   Title from cover.
   Continues: Western & English fashions.
   ISSN 1054-9323 = Equine business journal.
   1. Clothing trade—Periodicals.   2. Hat trade—Periodicals.
   3. Horse sports—Equipment and supplies—Periodicals.   I.
   Title: EBJ.
   WMLC L 83/9100   sf 90-92572
               r687—dc12a¬
                                     AACR 2
DLC

Equine veterinary education. — Vol. 1, no. 1 (Sept.
   1989)-   — Newmarket, Suffolk : R. & W.
   Publications, 1989-
       v. : ill. ; 29 cm.
   Quarterly.
   Title from cover.
   Established by British Equine Veterinary Association
   (BEVA).
   Other title: EVE
   ISSN 0957-7734.
   1. Veterinarians—Education—Periodicals.   2. Horses—
   Diseases—Periodicals.   3. Veterinary medicine—Periodi-
   cals.   4. Equine sports medicine—Periodicals.   I. British
   Equine Veterinary Association.   II. Title: EVE.
                                   sn 90-16630
                                   AACR 2
   CU-AM   NIC   PU   ViBIbV

frequently printed on only one side and posted as one might put up
notices on a bulletin board. Broadsheets are also generally involved with
one subject. Newsletters usually contain information supplied by one
person but on many subjects. Newsletters have been common since the
Roman times and are still an important source of information for the
researcher. Many corporations produce specific newsletters on various
topics. The Carnegie Foundation publishes a periodical newsletter with

reports on current research financed by the trust. One should not overlook this source when researching a topic.

Early newspapers were printed sporadically at first, gradually becoming more frequent, once or twice weekly. Some earliest newspapers left one page blank for the reader or subscriber to add news before passing the newspaper to someone else. Church and government official were quick to grasp the influence of newspapers, soon subjecting them to censorship, licensing, taxing and later bribery and prosecution of the editors, printers and writers (reporters). Copies of many early newspapers have survived and the newspapers of the last 350 to 400 years provide historical information, opinions of the times and other information not recorded elsewhere. Many early newspapers in Europe and in the United States invited writers to make unpaid contributions, thus becoming literary and political forums for the intellectuals. By the early 18th century, newspapers had become indispensable in politics and economics and continued to increase despite attempts by governments to control their number and content.

Newspapers in the 20th century have declined in numbers but individual papers have larger circulations. As costs increase, technology for production has become necessary for newspapers to survive. Most newspapers today are composed by computer and printed by photo-offset techniques developed since 1970. The new technology requires less staff and space for composing and printing.

Newspapers are read worldwide and are still a powerful influence on public opinion. They can build or destroy ideas, people or governments and range from the state-controlled propaganda sheets to the free press of the West. Debates about censorship continue. Western papers are expected to play a role in uncovering corruption and scandal, such as the role played by the newspapers in discovering the Watergate scandal. Modern newspapers provide services to researchers. Back issues are kept in a large collection, the "morgue," and are usually accessible to the consumer. Most newspapers also have a reference library that is used by the reporters and other staff preparing and editing articles. Large newspapers like the *New York Times* have comprehensive reference collections.

The type of information in newspapers falls into three general categories, (1) business and economic news, (2) governmental news, laws, politicians, elections and rulers and (3) social and neighborhood news. Newspapers are important sources of current information. Some are "newspapers of record" in that they print the full text of speeches, public notices and sometimes legislation. If the text of a speech by the governor of New York is needed it will be found in the *New York Times.*

Major newspapers are indexed. All important news and information in the *New York Times* is found by using the *New York Times Index.* The index lists the month, day, section number and page and column number. Other newspaper indexes use the same format. All contain subject entries and personal name entries with cross references. Be sure to check the abbreviations used and additional instructions at the beginning of the index. Library holdings of newspapers are generally on microfilm. For additional information see the section of Chapter 14 on nonprint materials. For additional information about newspapers check the catalog. For additional information about guides and directories, use subject headings guides (Chapter 2) or correct subject headings.

Exercises for Chapter 8

1. Check the card catalog for those subject headings pertinent to your major field of interest. List the indexes and abstracts in your library that relate to that field. If you do not find any listed in the catalog ask the reference librarian.
2. Check a guide to the literature in your major field of interest and record the titles of indexes and abstracts that are published but not available in your library. (Check *Guide to Reference Books* and other titles listed in Chapter 5.)
3. Check the catalog under the heading Periodicals — Directories; list the directories in your library with their call numbers.
4. Using the *Reader's Guide to Periodical Literature* (RGPL), v. 56, 1996, v. 44, 1984–1985, look up the subject Investment Fraud. Compare it to RGPL, v. 34, 1974–75 and v. 39, 1979–80 entries for Investment Fraud. Note subheadings and cross-referencing.
5. Using RGPL, recording the volume number and date, check the entries under the subject Iraq. Note the type of subheadings used and the "see" and "see also" references. Compare the entries for the years 1974–75, 1990–91, and 1996–97.
6. Check in the *Social Sciences Index, Business Periodicals Index* and *Education Index* under the subject heading Iraq. Record the title of index, volume number and year, type of subheadings and cross-references ("see" and "see also"). If your library does not have these indexes, check three other titles.

7. Look in the catalog for the subject card Periodicals. Record, with call numbers, those that may be useful, e.g. those listing periodical title abbreviations, bibliographies and indexes.

Important Terms in Chapter 8

Wilson Index	*union lists*
abstracts	*newsletters*
broadsheets	*Reader's Guide*
ULS	*RGPL*
NST	

Important Books for Chapter 8

DIRECTORIES

Directory of Electronic Journals, Newsletters, and Academic Discussion Lists. Washington, D.C.: Association of Research Libraries, Office of Scientific and Academic Publishing, 1991–.

Fry, Ronald W. *Magazines Career Directory: Guide to the Top U.S. and Canadian Magazine Publishers.* 4th rev. ed. Hawthorne, NJ: Career Press, 1990.

Katz, William Armstrong. *Magazines for Libraries: For the General Reader and School, Junior College and Public Library.* 9th ed. New York: R. R. Bowker, 1997.

Magazine Industry Market Place: The Directory of American Periodical Publishing. New York: R. R. Bowker, 1987.

Standard Periodical Directory, 1983–84, 13th ed. New York: Oxbridge Communications, 1990.

Ulrich's International Periodicals Directory. New York: R. R. Bowker, 1932–(yearly).

INDEXES AND ABSTRACTS

Abstracts in Anthropology. Westport, CT: Greenwood, v. 1– , 1970– .

Abstracts of English Studies, 1958– . Boulder, CO: National Council of Teachers of English, 1958– (monthly).

Art Index. New York: H. W. Wilson, v. 1– , 1929– .

Bibliography and Index of Geology. Alexandria, VA: American Geological

Institute, v. 32– , 1969– . Earlier volumes published under the title *Bibliography and Index of Geology Exclusive of North America.*

Business Periodicals Index, 1958– . New York: H. W. Wilson, 1958– (monthly).

Chemical Abstracts, 1907– . Columbus, OH: American Chemical Society, 107– (weekly).

Cumulative Index to Nursing and Allied Health Literature. Glendale, CA: Glendale Adventist Medical Center, v. 1– , 1956– . Earlier volumes have a slightly different title.

General Science Index. New York: H. W. Wilson, v. 1– , 1978– .

Historical Abstracts. Santa Barbara, CA: ABC Clio. V. 1– , 1955– . Beginning with v. 17, 1971 it is published in four parts per volume.

Humanities Index. New York: H. W. Wilson, v. 1– , 1971– . Earlier title was Social Sciences and Humanities Index, preceded by the International Index.

Index to Government Periodicals, 1970– . Chicago: Infodata International, 1970– (quarterly, with annual circulation).

The Magazine Index, 1977– . Belmont, CA: Information Access Corp., 1977– .

MLA International Bibliography of Books and Articles on the Modern Languages and Literature. New York: Modern Language Association of America, 1921– .

Pooles's Index to Periodical Literature. Reprinted. Gloucester, MA: Peter Smith, 1963. (7 vols. Covering 1802–1906.)

Psychological Abstracts, 1927– . Lancaster, PA: American Psychological Association, 1927– (monthly).

Reader's Guide to Periodical Literature, 1900– . New York: H. W. Wilson, 1900– (semi-monthly).

Recently Published Articles. Washington, DC: American Historical Review, v. 1– , 1976–1990. Formerly published as a section of the American Historical Review.

Social Science Citation Index. Philadelphia: Institute for Scientific Information, v. 1– , 1973– . The same publisher also issues *Science Citation Index* and *Arts and Humanities Citation Index.*

Social Sciences Index. New York: H. W. Wilson, v. 1– , 1974– . Earlier title was *Social Sciences and Humanities Index* which was preceded by International Index.

Sociological Abstracts. San Diego, CA: Sociological Abstracts, v. 1– , 1952– .

NEWSPAPER INDEXES

New York Times Index. New York: New York Times Co., 1913– . Earlier
series index the *New York Times* from September 18, 1951.

Personal Name Index to the New York Times Index, 1851–1974. Succa-
Sunna, NJ: Roxbury Data Interface, 1976. Supplements to main set
have been issued to 1989.

The Times Index. Reading, England: Newspaper Archive Developments,
1973– . 1790–1905 indexes as *Palmer's Index to the Times Newspaper.* Indexes to other years published by various publishers.

Wall Street Journal Index. New York: Dow Jones, 1958– . Starting in 1981,
the index includes *Barron's Index.*

Washington Post Index. Ann Arbor, MI: University Microfilms International, 1989– . Earlier volumes published by other publishers.

UNION LISTS

New Serials Titles. New York: R. R. Bowker. A union list of serials com-
mencing publication after December 31, 1949. Sets for the years
1950–1970 (4 vols.), 1971–1975 (2 vols.), 1976–1980 (2 vols.),
1981–1985 (6 vols.), 1986–1989, 1991–1995, 1996–1998 (6 vols.),
monthly, quarterly issues and annual volumes.

Union List of Serials in Libraries in the United States and Canada, 3d ed.
New York: H. W. Wilson, 1965 (5 vols.).

OTHER HELPFUL BOOKS

Alkire, Leland G., ed. *Periodical Title Abbreviations*, 11th ed. Detroit:
Gale Research, 1998. 3 vols.: v. 1 by abbreviations, v. 2 by titles,
v. 3 new periodical title abbreviations. Kept up to date by annual
supplement.

Kujoth, Jean Spealman. *Subject Guide to Periodical Indexes and Review
Indexes.* Metuchen, NJ: Scarecrow, 1969.

9. On-Line Database Searching, CD-ROM Indexes and Reference Sources

Objectives

After studying this chapter the student shall be able to
- Search on-line databases
- Use Boolean operators in constructing a search
- Search a CD-ROM
- Know how to access the Internet

General Information

Searching for specific types of information on the Internet is included in many earlier chapters. There are many ways to access the Internet. Your library may provide access via its OPAC. Many public libraries provide free access to the Internet from their OPAC in addition to direct connections to one or more of the specific services discussed below. Most academic library OPACs provide access to at least one of the following services in addition to other databases such as First-Search (chapter 14). Some of the databases discussed below may still be available in CD-ROM format but in general that format is being phased out and replaced with the on-line versions.

CD-ROM reference sources generally are available at a stand-alone workstation. A CD tower might be networked to several workstations creating a small local network. This network allows all the connected computers (workstations) access to all the CDs in the tower. Reference sources generally found in this format include phone books, encyclopedias or individual reference books (e.g. *Books in Print*).

Whether searching paper indexes, on-line indexes or CD-ROMs, students must remember that all periodical citations have equal import of value. Further students should discriminate in which citations to pursue. Students should also realize that the library pays a fee to provide access to these databases. If one wished to access these databases in a way other than via a library OPAC, charges would be incurred.

WILSONLINE, WILSONDISC, and Wilson Web

WILSONDISC is available in versions for DOS (PCs), Macintosh and Windows. As of 1997 the Mac and PC versions have 9 full text databases, 9 databases which included abstracts and 15 databases which are just indexes. The Windows version has 17 full text databases, 11 abstract databases and 15 index databases. These databases are some of the same indexes discussed in Chapter 8.

Each database entry includes the following data elements: subject heading; author; title; source; article title; year of publication and pagination. The kinds of searches available in each database depend on the individual database. Possible type of searches include: keyword; personal name (as author or subject); words in the title; journal title; words in the abstract; Dewey Decimal number; SIC code; year of publication; case name or citation; and statute name or citation.

Boolean operators can be used to narrow or broaden searches and truncation is permitted. Cross-references are included in the search results. Personal names are searched as BOTH subject and author unless otherwise specified. Names are inverted by the program unless the searcher specifies the name is not to be inverted. Names of organizations can be searched as a phrase. Searches can be modified, saved and a new search conducted on the same or another database.

Searching using command language rather than using menus is also possible. Command language searches would include words such as FIND, AND or NOT and could include truncation symbols such as #, !, $, ?, n (for neighbor), GET and EXPAND.

It's easy to be totally involved in on-line searching.

WILSONSEARCH differs from WILSONDISC as it is on-line (via a modem) and can retrieve more current citations. Each search requires a separate call to the WILSONSEARCH line. The WILSONDISC menu includes the option of continuing the search on WILSONLINE. Some libraries disable this function. Charges are incurred for each WILSON-LINE search. On-line searching also includes command language searches. Command language searches allow access to data elements such as physical descriptions (color, bibliographies, graphs, etc.). It is necessary to consult the list of stop words when constructing a command language search. Access to WILSONLINE is via the Internet, Sprintnet, TymNET, DATAPAC or telnet. Wilson charges for use of WILSONLINE depend on the individual library. It is possible to access WILSONLINE but setting up deposit accounts and determining charges is a complex matter. The Wilson company suggests that use of all its on-line products be through a library.

WILSONDISC for Windows screens include button bars and menu bars. Clicking on icons provides access to pull down menus, functions and other screens. On-line help includes information on using truncation and wildcards; searching hyphenated phrases; and Boolean searches using AND, WITH, NEAR, OR and NOT. Some databases include a thesaurus, which can be searched. Searches can be saved, modified and reused.

WilsonWeb has the same number and types of databases as WILSONDISC plus a Director/Authority file to the Wilson Journal Directory. WilsonWeb is the retrieval system available on the World Wide Web. Each database has a dataguide with information about that specific database. Consulting the guide before starting a search is advisable. Types of searches available include: subject; phrases; numbers; indexed field (such as author, article title, etc.); thesaurus for that database; use of Boolean operators; truncation and wildcards; and limit field operators (by specific date or time period). Records can be marked for downloading and sorting of records is also possible.

These Wilson products provide the ability to design complex searches and a careful reading of the instructions before starting to search is advised. For more information about Boolean search design and use of Boolean operators, see the following section on SilverPlatter.

SilverPlatter

SilverPlatter databases are searched with software known as SPIRS (SilverPlatter Information Retrieval System). This software has versions for Windows, DOS, Macintosh, UNIX, and the World Wide Web. Some of the most useful searching features include:

1. searching multiple databases simultaneously with a single search statement
2. free text search an entire database
3. refine a search using controlled index terms
4. use of Boolean AND, OR, NOT, WITH, NEAR, ADJ
5. wildcards for alternate or unknown spelling
6. combining searches

Other searching features are also included.

The databases available have been grouped by subjects and include: Business; Education; Environment; Food and Agriculture; General Reference; Health and Safety; Humanities; Life Sciences; Medical; Public Affairs; Science and Technology; and Social Sciences. A library may subscribe to one or more of the available database groups.

The Boolean operators provided include more choices than some other databases and OPACS. The operators WITH, NEAR and ADJ (adjacent) can be useful in narrowing a search. The use of NEAR usually accompanied by a number means that the search terms must appear within that number of words of each other. The ADJ operator means the words are adjacent or next to each other. Using these operators makes it much easier to find a specific phrase or multiword term. It is more efficient search than using AND which will identify all the entries that include all the search terms. When searching for articles on blue jays a search using ADJ or NEAR/1 as operators would produce the best results. If the search construction were *Blue AND Jay* the results would likely produce results containing unrelated articles. A search for *Blue NEAR/2 Jay* or *Blue ADJ Jay* is likely to produce a better result.

It is also possible to combine several searches. Each search is assigned a number (in order conducted), e.g. #1, #2, #3,... #10. A sample search to find articles about apple trees might appear as

Search	Term	Citations
#1	apple	50
#2	tree	1000
#3	#1 AND #2	10 (with both terms)
#4	fruit	75
#5	#2 NEAR/3 #4	16 (terms within 3 words of each other)

A search could be broadened by including the term OR.

#6	#2 OR #4	1075 (either term)

To review, a search may be narrowed by using AND to find two (2) or more words or terms in the same *record*. A search is widened by using OR. NEAR means terms must appear in the same *field* thus a narrower search than using AND.

Wildcard searching is also available. This allows the use of characters such as !, ? or * to replace letter(s) in the search term. This is useful if the correct spelling is unknown or there are variant forms of the term. Wildcards enable the searcher to conduct one rather than several searches. It will be necessary to read the directions or consult the help screen for directions on the use of wildcards for a specific database.

SPIRS also provides hotlinks between records and will identify journals held in the library. Bibliographic information and/or full text may be printed or downloaded to a disk. Manipulation of downloaded records with a word processor is also available. If your library subscribes

Sometimes it takes a group to learn all the features of a database.

to SilverPlatter products, check with the librarian on the library's policy for printing and downloading to a disk.

InfoTrac

InfoTrac, a product from Information Access Corporation (IAC) may also be referred to as Searchbank. The libraries that subscribe to the Searchbank service generally provide access via the OPAC. The company is phasing out CD-ROM. A nice feature of this family of databases is that most citations include the full text. In the fall of 1998 IAC, the Gale Corporation and several other companies have merged and will be known as the Gale Group.

Available databases include various periodical indexes, newspaper indexes, company profiles and individual reference books. The back files of each database vary from the mid 1970s to the early 1990s. Some databases, such as Expanded Academic Index ASAP include most subject areas (Astronomy, Religion, Law, History, Psychology, Humanities, Current Events, Sociology, Communications and General Science). Others, such as Health Reference Center are more narrowly focused (Fitness, Pregnancy, Medicine, Nutrition, Disease, Public Health, Occupational Health and Safety, Alcohol and Drug Abuse, HMOs, Prescription Drugs, etc.). Other databases available in 1999 include: Expanded Academic Index (in several versions), Newsletters ASAP, SuperTOM, Health Reference Center (in several versions), General BusinessFile ASAP, Gen'l Reference Center (in several versions), PrimaryTOM, National Newspaper Index, CPI.Q (Canadian focus), Business-Company Profiles, Peterson's Graduate Programs, Peterson's Undergraduate Guide, Business Index ASAP, Investext, Computer Database, LegalTrac, F&S IndexPlus Text-U.S., predicts PROMPT, European Business ASAP, Compendex, *Sociological Abstracts*, SIRS Researcher, *Books in Print*, Pro CD Phone, *PAIS International* and *ISI Current Contents*.

Searching can be done at several levels. EasyTrac provides a simple searching technique. Just type the word(s) to be searched in the entry box and click on [Search]. If the search produces numerous entries a display will list all subjects in which the word(s) occur and the number of citations indexed under each. Just click on the desired items to access the citations. Key word searching is also available by selecting *key word* rather than *subject*. The menu bar at the top of the screen provides choices such as new search, new database, switch to PowerTrac, Help, citation list, article and mark list. Under the menu bar and above the citation list is a search reference number, e.g., R1, R2, etc. These are useful in refining a search in PowerTrac. Next to each citation is a box to mark the citation for later retrieval and/or printing of the full text. Keywords searched appear in red. To retrieve the full text of an article, click on the word VIEW (in blue).

PowerTrac provides different access points in the databases. In addition you can use Boolean operators such as AND, NOT and OR when constructing a search. You can also combine previous searches using the "R" number (e.g., R1 AND R3 NOT R2). Range operators are also available (e.g., BEFORE October 1998). For additional instructions for using either EasyTrac or PowerTrac click on the Help box.

The citation format begins with the article title followed by the author's name, journal title (in italics), date, volume number, issue number, beginning page number and number of pages in the article in parenthesis.

Be sure to note the icons on the screen that help navigate a citation list or full text of an article. At the end of the full text is the article number (e.g., Article 12345). For additional information visit the InfoTrac site at www.infotrac.com.

The option of printing articles or downloading to your own disk will depend on the policy of your library. Some libraries charge for printing (a per page charge) and others might restrict the number of free pages you can print. Be sure to check with the librarian on your library's policy.

ProQuest Direct

UMI's ProQuest Direct is a database of articles originally published in magazines, newspapers and journals. It will be found on the OPAC of those libraries subscribing to the service. Some libraries also make it available to their borrowers on the World Wide Web. It is necessary to enter an ID or bar code number to gain access when searching from a computer not in the library.

There are three basic searching methods and two levels for each method. Methods of searching are by *word*, *topic* and *publication* and levels are *basic* and *advanced*. Searches are not case sensitive. When a search is entered a list of articles matching the search will be displayed. The list is headed by a number, R1, R2,...R10. This is the *result list*.

Clicking on an article will display it on the screen. Articles may be added to your personal *marked list* by selecting it from either the *result list* or when the article is displayed on the screen.

Select either *basic* or *advanced* before beginning a search. To do a basic search by *word* just enter the word(s) in the text box and click on [search]. Choosing options on the screen, such as current, backfile or selecting only one database may narrow searches. When no selections are made, ProQuest uses the preset defaults to provide the broadest possible search. When doing a *word* search *advanced* a series of dropdown menus and four text boxes will be displayed. Look through the dropdown menus and construct a search. The menus provide Boolean operators and different indexing fields to choose from. Enter the word(s) to be searched and click on [search]. Available Boolean operators include AND, OR, AND NOT, WITHIN, PRECEDE BY, and WITHIN DOC. See the help screens for specific instructions on the use of these operators. Indexed fields include: author, source, subject terms, personal name, company name, article text, article type, and source type. See the help screens for detailed information on each of these fields. The *article type* field is interesting, as searches can be limited to such things as a review, speech or interview. Range restrictors (dates) are also available.

The search options also automatically look for spelling variants and plurals. If selected, ProQuest will also search for synonyms and other words conceptually related to the search. Check the help pages for additional searching hints, such as how to use truncation, wildcards, caption fields and parentheses ().

Article type searching narrows the search and identifies only specific types of articles desired. For example the search could be limited to finding only poetry, editorials, interviews or reviews. Consult the help file for a complete list of *article type* fields.

A *search by publication* is used to find a specific issue of a specific magazine, newspaper or journal. To conduct this type of search, be sure to click on *for publication* before entering the search.

To *search by topic* be sure to click on *by topic* before entering a search. Enter word(s) or phrase and click on search. ProQuest will display a list, which matches the topics entered. Browse the list and click on the desired topic(s). Click on *search now* to look for articles about the selected topic.

Articles are available in five (5) formats: citation, abstract, full text, full text + graphics, and page image. The displayed format may be determined by publisher's copyrights and/or your library's contract with UMI.

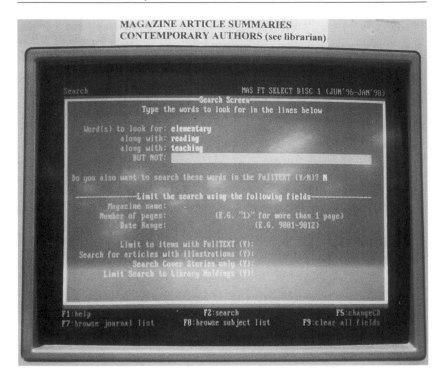

Ebsco's CD-ROM version of Magazine Article Summaries.

ProQuest provides excellent help screens with examples and explanations. Be sure to consult help for suggestions when constructing any advanced searches.

EBSCO

Ebsco is a subscription service used by many libraries. They provide indexing, abstracts and full text of journals. The database contains more than 260,000 titles. Their CD-ROM Magazine Articles Summaries was quite popular. That service is being replaced with an on-line version.

Searching can be done using author, journal titles, publisher, date or range of dates, keywords and full text index. Once articles are identified the display includes an abstract as well as the bibliographic citation. Links to the full text are available when the library has a subscription to that title or if the article appears in a sample issue. Browsing the table of contents of a specific journal is also available.

An added feature is *journal details* pages. Users will find a description of the journal, editorial guidelines for manuscript submission and the web resources of related interest.

Academic Abstracts (*FullText Elite*, *FullText Ultra*, *Academic Search Select* and *Academic Search Plus*) is one that might be found on an academic OPAC. The number of full text journals included in these products range from 160 (*Elite*) to 825 (*Academic Search Plus*). The number of journal titles indexed range from 930 to over 3,000. *ERIC*, *PAIS International*, *PsychLIT*, and *World Magazine Bank* are examples of the more than 60 databases available from Ebsco. For additional information, visit Ebsco's web at www.epnet.com.

LANs—Local Area Network

The term LANs is used when computers are linked together, often by a main frame computer. The linking allows all connected computers to access the same databases. Many libraries use this technique to allow many simultaneous users access to the same CD-ROMs. Only those computers so linked will have access to the CD-ROMs.

Commercial Vendors of Databases

In addition to the services described above, there are some databases available only through vendors that charge per search or per citation displayed/printed. The charges may also include connect time plus long distance phone charges. DIALOG, BRS and Lexis/Nexis are among the more commonly used suppliers. The vendor assigns a password for access to the database and bills are sent monthly or charged to a deposit account or credit card. Vendors provide regularly updated instructions for searching databases they supply. Most users of these services are corporations and professionals (e.g., lawyers). Some colleges and universities have an educational password to Lexis/Nexis, allowing students and faculty access to most of their extensive legal databases. For this access the schools pays a preset monthly fee. Searching in BRS and DIALOG and other similar services may be available at your library. Ask the librarian if these services are available and what the charges would be. Most schools providing this service require that the librarian do the actual searching.

Searching or Surfing the Net

As mentioned above, some libraries provide access to the Internet from their OPAC's. Individuals may also access the Internet from their personal computer. The method of accessing the Internet is a personal choice. Local companies may provide access or one may choose a large corporate provider (AOL, MSN, WebTV, etc.). All providers charge a fee for access to the "Net." A web browser is necessary for searching the Internet. Many browsers are available, often at no cost. Popular browsers include NetScape and Microsoft Internet Explorer. Some browsers and Internet access providers include telnet as an option. Telnet is generally needed to access college and university library catalogs (see Chapter 3). Many Internet sites provide menus enabling the user to find information easily. Yahoo and AltaVista are popular sites that continually add and update sources and information. Some sites such as Yahoo also provide free e-mail accounts.

Exercises for Chapter 9

1. What CD-ROM products does your library subscribe to? Is there a printer attached?
2. Does your library provide on-line database searching? Who does the searching? Is there a charge?
3. Does your library provide access to the Internet on the OPAC?
4. Look up the subjects checked for other indexes. See exercises for Chapter 8. (Iraq, investment fraud, memory)

Important Terms for Chapter 9

WILSONDISC	*Downloading*
Infotrac	*IAC*
WILSONLINE	*Yahoo*
BRS	*AOL*
DIALOG	*Web browser*
SilverPlatter	*WilsonWeb*
Ebsco	*AltaVista*
Boolean	*ProQuest*
Vendor	*LANs*

Important Books for Chapter 9

Database Directory. White Plains, NY: Knowledge Industry Publications, 1984– . Directory of "databases accessible online in North America."

Directory of Portable Databases. New York: Cuadra Elsvier, 1990– . Semi-annual, v. 1, no. 1– . January 1990.

Frey, Donnalyn, and Rick Adams. *!%@, A Directory of Electronic Mail Addresses and Networks*. 2nd ed. rev. and updated. Sebastopol, CA: O'Reilly and Associates, 1990.

Gould, Cheryl. *Searching Smart on the World Wide Web: Tools and Techniques for Getting Quality Results*. Berkeley, CA: Library Solutions Press, 1998.

LaQuey, Tracy L. *The User's Directory of Computer Networks*. Bedford, MA: Digital Press, 1990.

Online Database Search Services Directory: A Reference and Referral Guide to Libraries, Information Firms and Other Sources Providing Computerized Information Retrieval and Associated Services Using Publically Available Online Databases. John Schmittroth, Jr., and Doris Morris Maxfield, eds. Detroit, MI: Gale Research, 1984– .

Want, Robert S. *How to Search the Web: A Quick Reference Guide to Finding Things on the World Wide Web*. New York: Want Pub., 1998.

10. Literature and Criticism

Objectives

After studying this chapter the student shall be able to
- locate poems, short stories and other forms of literature published in anthologies and periodicals
- find critical analyses of plays, poems, short stories, novels and speeches
- identify and record the indexes of literary forms owned by the library
- locate plot summaries

General Information

Literary forms include plays, poems, short stories, novels and speeches. Obviously, there are many items that one might want to retrieve. Finding one poem may be difficult or impossible if one only uses the catalog. Students will find the task less demanding if they consult a special catalog, anthology or index. Poems, short stories and essays are usually published in collections called anthologies or in subject-specific periodicals. Anthologies may include the works of one or multiple authors. The scope is determined by the editor. With practice the student will find anthologies by using the catalog. Correct subject headings are essential to seeking materials. The subject heading books (see Chapter 4) provide alternate headings useful in this task. For example, to locate a particular play, the correct heading is drama, not plays. With some practice one will learn key subject headings and no longer need to consult the book each time a subject heading is needed. Besides using anthologies, the student will use alternative research sources, such as indexes, catalogs and abstracts.

Indexes and Catalogs

The *Short Story Index* (Figure 10.1), published by the H. W. Wilson Company, is a guide to locating short stories that have been published in collections. The index lists the stories by author's name, title and subject, and all entries are in one alphabet. Also it identifies the book or periodical title in which the story appeared. For example, Bowen's story "Human Habitation" is in the collection Oxford Book of Travel Stories edited by P. Craig. The format is typical "Wilson" format (see Chapter 8). This index is extremely comprehensive and should be sufficient for most purposes.

Short Story Criticism is an introduction to major short story writers of all eras and nationalities. The editors have chosen the most important published criticism. Each volume includes 8-10 authors and each entry reflects the amount of critical attention the author has received. The chosen criticisms are from English language publications or foreign critics in translation. Each entry includes biographical and critical introduction; a list of principal works in chronological order; criticism; bibliographical citations and additional readings. Cumulative index for authors, titles and nationalities is included in each volume.

The Essay and General Literature Index is a guide to essays and short articles published in books rather than periodicals. For information about an author, one looks under the author's name. There are also subject headings to provide access to items when an author's name is unknown to the student. Figure 10.2 is a typical entry. The author's name, James, heads the entry. In the center of the column, the term "about" shows that the items under this heading are articles about Henry James — biographical information, but not articles written by him. The first item is by M. Bradbury, titled "The lighted stage: Twain, James and the European stage" in a collection by M. Bradbury, *Dangerous Pilgrimages* on pages 159-202. Further down the column the heading appears in the center, "About individual works." Under this heading are articles about *The American, The American scene, The awkward age,* etc. For complete information about anthologies indexed in *Essay and General Literature Index,* see the back of each volume.

Figure 10.1 Short Story Index

Borofka, David, 1954—*Continued*
  The blue cloak
    Borofka, D. Hints of his mortality
  The children's crusade
    Borofka, D. Hints of his mortality
  The girl on the highway
    Borofka, D. Hints of his mortality
  Hints of his mortality
    Borofka, D. Hints of his mortality
  Mid-Clair
    Borofka, D. Hints of his mortality
  Reflected music
    Borofka, D. Hints of his mortality
  The sisters
    Borofka, D. Hints of his mortality
  Strays
    Borofka, D. Hints of his mortality
  The summers of my sex
    Borofka, D. Hints of his mortality
  Tabloid news
    Borofka, D. Hints of his mortality
  The whole lump
    Borofka, D. Hints of his mortality
Borovsky's hollow woman. Kress, N., and
  Duntemann, J.
Borrowed scenery. Mazur, G. D.
BOSNIA AND HERCEGOVINA
          Sarajevo
  Davetian, B. The forbidden zone
BOSTON (MASS.) *See* Massachusetts—Boston
BOSWELL, JAMES, 1740-1795
          About
  De la Torre, L. The bedlam bam
BOTANISTS
  Barrett, A. The littoral zone
Both definitions of save. Goldbarth, A.
Bots: a love story and a dream. Hemmingson, M.
BOTSWANA
  Head, B. The collector of treasures
A bottle of Perrier. Wharton, E.
Bottom. Bishop, B.
Boucher, Anthony, 1911-1968
  Crime must have a stop
    The Oxford book of American detective sto-
      ries; ed. by T. Hillerman and R. Herbert
  The last hand
    Win, lose or die; ed. by C. Manson and C.
      Scarborough
Bound [excerpt] Swissa, A.
Bounty. Saunders, G.
Bourke, Angela
  The back way home
    Bourke, A. By salt water
  Beauty treatment
    Bourke, A. By salt water
  Blue murder
    Bourke, A. By salt water
  Camouflage
    Bourke, A. By salt water
  Charm
    Bourke, A. By salt water
  Deep down
    Bourke, A. By salt water
  Dreams of sailing
    Bourke, A. By salt water
  Ham
    Bourke, A. By salt water
  Lemon grass
    Bourke, A. By salt water

  Majella's quilt
    Bourke, A. By salt water
  Mayonnaise to the hills
    Bourke, A. By salt water
  Nesting
    Bourke, A. By salt water
  Ohio by the ocean
    Bourke, A. By salt water
  Pinkeens
    Bourke, A. By salt water
  Secret passages
    Bourke, A. By salt water
  Le soleil et le vent
    Bourke, A. By salt water
  The whale in the garden
    Bourke, A. By salt water
Bova, Ben, 1932-
  Inspiration
    Nebula awards 30
  Risk assessment
    The Williamson effect; ed. by R. Zelazny
BOW AND ARROW *See* Archery
Bowels Jones. Richards, A.
Bowen, Elizabeth, 1899-1973
  Human habitation
    The Oxford book of travel stories; ed. by P.
      Craig
  A love story
    The Oxford book of English love stories; ed.
      by J. Sutherland
Bowler, Michael
  The last season
    Writers' week; ed. by D. Marcus
Bowles, Paul, 1910-
  Allal
    American gothic tales; ed. by J. C. Oates
BOWLING
  Bell, C. Mercy
Boxes. Griner, P.
BOXING
  McCann, C. Step we gaily, on we go
  Norris, L. A big night
  Norris, L. The Brighton Midgets
  Piglia, R. Mousy Benitez sang boleros
  Rice, D. Empty corner
A boy asks a question. Barnes, D.
The boy at Pydew. Beagan, G.
Boy born with tattoo of Elvis. Butler, R. O.
Boy on a train. Ellison, R.
The boy orator. Daugherty, T.
BOY SCOUTS
  Davenport, G. The river
  Ing, D. Eagles
  Williamson, J. Jamboree
The boy who took off in a tree. Balcells, J.
Boyd, William, 1952-
  Loose continuity
    The New Yorker v72 p76-80+ F 19 '96
Boyers, Robert
  In hiding
    Michigan Quarterly Review v35 p499-12
      Summ '96
  Torso
    Southwest Review v81 p90-106 Wint '96
Boyfriend. Diaz, J.
Boyle, T. Coraghessan
  Killing babies
    The New Yorker v72 p86-90+ D 2 '96

Figure 10.2   Essay and General Literature Index

James, Henry, 1843-1916

About

Bradbury, M. The lighted stage: Twain, James and the European shrine. (*In* Bradbury, M. Dangerous pilgrimages p158-202)

Cowley, M. The two Henry Jameses. (*In* Cowley, M. New England writers and writing p105-13)

Ozick, C. What Henry James knew. (*In* Ozick, C. Fame & folly p101-28)

Wilson, E. Henry James. (*In* Wilson, E. From the uncollected Edmund Wilson p23-34)

Wilson, E. Magazine stories by masters: Faulkner, Edith Wharton, and James. (*In* Wilson, E. From the uncollected Edmund Wilson p342-48)

About individual works

The American

Tuttleton, J. W. The marrying kind: James's The American. (*In* Tuttleton, J. W. Vital signs p104-23)

The American scene

Wilson, E. Henry James and Auden in America. (*In* Wilson, E. From the uncollected Edmund Wilson p329-35)

The awkward age

McWhirter, D. What's awkward about The awkward age? (*In* Centuries' ends, narrative means; ed. by R. D. Newman p212-21)

The complete plays

Wilson, E. Henry James's The complete plays. (*In* Wilson, E. From the uncollected Edmund Wilson p336-39)

The Europeans

Tuttleton, J. W. Propriety and fine perception: James's The Europeans. (*In* Tuttleton, J. W. Vital signs p124-43)

The liar

Lane, C. Framing fears, reading designs: the homosexual art of painting in James, Wilde, and Beerbohm. (*In* Lane, C. The ruling passion p72-98)

Bibliography

Zacharias, G. W. Henry James. (*In* American literary scholarship, 1994 p111-26)

James, Trevor, 1947-

"Telling our own stories": reclaiming difference, a Maori resistance to postculturalism. (*In* Cross-addressing; ed. by J. C. Hawley p51-65)

James, William, 1842-1910

About

Hassan, I. H. Imagination and belief: Wallace Stevens and William James. (*In* Hassan, I. H. Rumors of change p120-25)

Jameson, Fredric

Postmodernism and consumer society. (*In* Movies and mass culture; ed. by J. Belton p185-202)

About

Goldstein, J. L. The female aesthetic community. (*In* The Traffic in culture; ed. by G. E. Marcus and F. R. Myers p310-29)

Walsh, M. Jameson and "global aesthetics". (*In* Post-theory; ed. by D. Bordwell and N. Carroll p481-500)

Jameson, J. Franklin (John Franklin), 1859-1937

About individual works

The American Revolution considered as a social movement

Rothberg, M. John Franklin Jameson and the creation of The American Revolution considered as a social movement. (*In* The Transforming hand of revolution; ed. by R. Hoffman and P. J. Albert p1-26)

Young, A. F. American historians confront "the transforming hand of revolution". (*In* The Transforming hand of revolution, ed. by R. Hoffman and P. J. Albert p346-492)

Jameson, John Franklin *See* Jameson, J. Franklin (John Franklin), 1859-1937

Jameson's Raid, 1895-1896

Taylor, A. J. P. The Jameson Raid. (*In* Taylor, A. J. P. From the Boer War to the Cold War p33-35)

Jamieson, Sandra

The united colors of multiculturalism: rereading composition textbooks in the 90s. (*In* Mainstream(s) and margins; ed. by M. Morgan and S. Leggett p62-84)

Janes, Regina, 1946-

Danton does not sing La Marseillaise: Andrzej Wajda, Jean Renoir, and their French Revolutions. (*In* Studies in eighteenth-century culture v25 p293-307)

Janeway, Elizabeth

About individual works

Cross sections from a decade of change

Kizer, C. What women really do not want Elizabeth Janeway. (*In* Kizer, C. Picking and choosing p7-12)

Janicaud, Dominique, 1937-

The question of subjectivity in Heidegger's Being and time. (*In* Deconstructive subjectivities; ed. by S. Critchley and P. Dews p47-57)

Jankowski, Theodora A.

"The scorne of savage people": virginity as "forbidden sexuality" in John Lyly's Love's metamorphosis. (*In* Renaissance drama [1993] p123-53)

Japan

Civilization

Pfeiffer, K. L. The black hole of culture: Japan, radical otherness, and the disappearance of difference (or, "in Japan everything normal"). (*In* The Translatability of cultures; ed. by S. Budick and W. Iser p186-203)

1945-

Hassan, I. H. Japan and the United States: the burden of mutual perception. (*In* Hassan, I. H. Rumors of change p228-41)

Japanese aesthetics *See* Aesthetics, Japanese

Japanese American literature (English) *See* American literature—Japanese American authors

Japanese fiction

20th century

History and criticism

Napier, S. J. The magic of identity: magic realism in modern Japanese fiction. (*In* Magical realism; ed. by L. P. Zamora and W. B. Faris p451-75)

Speeches and plays are indexed in respective volumes. *The Speech Index*, edited by Robert Sutton, has been enlarged several times and is comprehensive. The *Play Index*, another Wilson index, is arranged in the typical format with the plays arranged by subject, author and title in one alphabet. The entries include information such as the number of acts, the number of male and female roles, the number of scenes, and in which collection the plays appear.

The *Fiction Catalog* (Figure 10.3) is also published by Wilson. It is one of the few sources that provides an index to novels by subject. If a novel about the Revolutionary War is needed, a check of the *Fiction Catalog* would provide a list of novels by authors and titles about the Revolutionary War. The *Fiction Catalog* gives book reviews for many novels listed. There are additional catalogs to "fictions by special subject," such as science fiction or mysteries.

Grangers Index to Poetry is a selective index to poems that appear in generally accessible collections. There are several editions that include many anthologies published over the years. A poem may be located by using the author index, the subject index, or the title or first line index. The preface of the *Poetry Index Annual* declares that it "has been developed to provide access to the preponderance of anthologized poetry which is not indexed anywhere." It also claims to be the "only work to systematically index *all* anthologies as they are published." The dictionary format provides entries by author, title and subject.

Criticism and Interpretation

Articles concerning literary works may be found by using the catalog, periodical indexes and explicators. When using the catalog look for the subheadings Criticism and Interpretation. For example, Stevenson, Robert Louis 1859–1895 — Criticism and Interpretation.

An explicator is a bibliography of articles about a literary work. Most explicators are specific, e.g. the poetry explication. There are guides, histories and dictionaries available for forms of literature. Concordances are also available for many authors and for specific works, such as the Bible. A concordance lists and locates all uses of specific words by an author in either his or her entire output or just in one or more works. There are also many books that can be consulted to help identify a quotation, such as *Bartlett's Familiar Quotations*. Most of these have subject and keyword indexes besides author indexes.

Figure 10.3 Fiction Catalog

Thomas, D. M.

Lady with a laptop; a novel. Carroll & Graf Pubs. 1996 246p $22

ISBN 0-7867-0308-3   LC 96-14409

"Simon Hopkins, a decidedly second-rate novelist whose most recently published work has quickly found its way to the remainder bin, has hired on for two weeks as leader of a writing workshop at an equally second-rate holistic holiday center on a minor Greek island. . . . As Simon's group begins to work on variations of a rather prurient murder mystery, reality intrudes in the form of an actual death—determined to be a suicide in the interests of bureaucratic simplicity but about which many questions remain. Thomas's remorseless but gentle caricaturing of New Age types and their struggles to remain 'politically correct' in the face of real-world situations makes for a marvelous reading." Libr J

Tilghman, Christopher

Mason's retreat. Random House 1996 290p $22

ISBN 0-679-42712-0   LC 95-4716

Also available Thorndike Press large print edition

The "title refers to an estate on Maryland's Eastern Shore that Edward Mason inherits from a maiden aunt and to which he brings his impoverished family in 1937. Edward, a confirmed Anglophile, has lived in England since 1923, but increasing debts have forced him to leave his small manufacturing firm in the hands of its foreman and return to America. To him it seems provincial and barren, but his wife and eldest son hope to make their home there." Libr J

The author "elegantly evokes both the physical landscape and the hermetic society and inbred culture of the Chesapeake Bay area. . . . In supple and beautifully inflected prose, he makes astute observations about the enduring blight of racism, the fallibility of human nature, the sacrifice of children as hostages to fortune and the inevitability of retribution—all conveyed with an illuminating, unflinching but compassionate eye." Publ Wkly

Topor, Tom, 1938-

The codicil; a novel. Hyperion 1994 338p $21.95

ISBN 0-7868-6153-3   LC 94-36986

"To the displeasure and disbelief of a deceased millionaire's widow and three kids, their late husband/father added a codicil to his will bequeathing half of his considerable estate to a child he fathered in Vietnam—if the youngster can be found alive. The estate attorneys hire Adam Bruno, a criminal lawyer turned detective, to locate Matthew Marshall's child, as the will dictates, hoping that he'll fumble the assignment." Publ Wkly

"The story is told in lean, precise, unsentimental prose that avoids cliché. The author, a former newspaperman, writes like a skilled reporter, never editorializing, dispassionately recounting some of the horrors of the sad American venture into Vietnam." N Y Times Book Rev

Tremaine, Jennie *See* Chesney, Marion

Trevor, William, 1928-

After rain; stories. Viking 1996 212p $22.95

ISBN 0-670-87007-2   LC 96-17282

Analyzed in Short story index

Contents: The piano tuner's wives; A friendship; Timothy's birthday; Child's play; A bit of business; After rain; Widows; Gilbert's mother; The potato dealer; Lost ground; A day; Marrying Damian

Each story in this "collection turns on lying, concealment or unbridled truthtelling; and these dislodging faults in the texture of reality are linked with cruelties ranging from mere spite to fraud, sectarian violence and murder." N Y Times Book Rev

Trollope, Joanna

The choir. Random House 1995 261p $22

ISBN 0-679-44454-8   LC 95-11612

First published 1993 in the United Kingdom

"The all-boy choir at Aldminster Cathedral is blessed with a cheerfully ferocious choirmaster, a magnificent seventeenth-century organ, and a celestial new treble in the earthly guise of eleven-year-old Henry Ashworth. But the choir also costs the diocese more than fifty thousand pounds a year, which the dean thinks might be better spent elsewhere—on new lighting, perhaps—and a delicious cathedral-town battle about tradition and privilege ensues. Almost all the characters in this companionable novel are on speaking terms with God, but His will, while frequently consulted, is variously interpreted." New Yorker

Truman, Margaret, 1924-

Murder at the National Gallery. Random House 1995 340p $23

ISBN 0-679-43530-1   LC 95-7089

This mystery features Annabel and Mac Smith. "As the National Gallery prepares for a special Caravaggio exhibit, senior curator Luther Mason happens to 'discover' a lost Caravaggio masterpiece while in Italy. Installing the original in the exhibit but making plans to replace it afterwards, Mason, aided by cultural attaché Carlo Giliberti, commissions two forgeries—one to send back to Italy and the other to sell to an underground art dealer who believes he is buying the original." Publ Wkly

"One of Truman's best efforts, this novel combines excitement, entertainment, and suspense with solid writing and creative plotting." Booklist

Tryon, Thomas

Night magic; [by] Tom Tryon. Simon & Schuster 1995 286p $23

ISBN 0-684-80393-3   LC 94-45654

"While performing in front of the Metropolitan Museum of Art, magician/mime Michael Hawke innocently draws Max Wurlitzer into his act. Unbeknownst to Michael, Max is not only a magician of some renown but also a practitioner of 'night magic,' the dark arts. Adopted by Max as his protégé, Michael soon finds that his overriding ambition may have dangerous consequences." Libr J

"Tryon's Faustian tale of the young hero's initiation and indoctrination is certain to be popular with occult fans." Booklist

Tyler, Anne, 1941-

Ladder of years. Knopf 1995 325p $24

ISBN 0-679-44155-7   LC 94-38909

This novel's protagonist is forty-year-old Delia Grinstead. "feeling unappreciated and unnoticed by her husband, a family doctor who took over Delia's father's practice, and increasingly unnecessary in the lives of her nearly grown children, Delia wanders off during a family beach vacation and starts a new life in a small town. She's sad and uncertain about her break with her previous life but oddly determined." Libr J

"'Ladder of Years' feels, indeed, like the story of a woman who thought she could prune her life down to a short story, only to find it blooming, unexpectedly, into an Anne Tyler novel. There can be few more delightful revelations." New Yorker

U

Unsworth, Barry, 1930-

The hide. Norton 1996 c1970 192p $22

ISBN 0-393-03955-2   LC 96-1915

First published 1970 in the United Kingdom

"Set in England, the novel has two narrators: 20-year-old Josh, a booth worker at a fair who idolizes and seeks approval from his manipulative, sexually predatory, more experienced coworker Mortimer; and much older, isolated, antisocial Simon, who lives

To locate reviews of movies, plays, television shows or other performances, follow the same general procedure used for finding book reviews. Reviews are most likely to be found in newspapers and periodicals and the subject headings should name the type of performance: Moving Pictures — Reviews. Libraries have not gotten around to using the simpler terms Films or Movies. To find plot summaries, use the catalog or check to see if the library owns some Magill sets, such as *Masterplot*. These sets include the characters in the story plus a short summary of the plot. They are not adequate substitutes for reading the work but may help to refresh the memory.

Remember, before using an unfamiliar index, guide, bibliography or other reference tool, read the introductory information to figure out the organization of the work, included or excluded materials, and scope or other limitations of the work being consulted.

Exercises for Chapter 10

1. Using the catalog, identify and record the indexes of various literary forms owned by your library.
2. Using the general information in this chapter and using what you have learned in earlier chapters, answer the following questions. List the sources used to answer the questions.
   (A) Where can you find a copy of the poem "Two dogs have I" by Ogden Nash?
   (B) Find the titles and locations of three short stories written by Mark Twain.
   (C) Find two book reviews of *Hunt for Red October* by Tom Clancy.
   (D) Locate two reviews of the movie *Hunt for Red October*.
   (E) Find three plays written by Neil Simon including productions for stage, radio and television. Locate the reviews for one of them.
   (F) Find an analysis or criticism of two works by Mark Twain.
   (G) Find a plot summary of a novel by James Fenimore Cooper.

Important Terms in Chapter 10

concordance   anthology
explicator

Important Books for Chapter 10

Adams, W. Davenport. *Dictionary of English Literature: Being a Comprehensive Guide to English Authors and Their Works*, 2d ed. London: Casall, Petter and Galpin, 1966.

American Poetry Index: An Author and Title Index to Poetry by Americans in Single Author Collections. V. 1- , 1981–82, ed. by Editorial Board, Granger Book Co. Great Neck, NY: Granger, 1988.

Bartlett, John. *Familiar Quotations: A Collection of Passages, Phrases, and Proverbs Traced to Their Sources in Ancient and Modern Literature.* Ed. by Emily Morrison Beck and the editorial staff of Little, Brown and Company. Boston: Little Brown, 1980. Fifteenth and 125th anniversary ed. rev. and enl.

Bloomfield, Masse. *How to Use a Library: A Guide to Literature Searching.* 2nd ed. Gilsum, NH: Masefield Books, 1991.

Carruth, Gorton, and Eugene Ehrlich. *The Harper Book of American Quotations.* New York: Harper & Row, 1988.

Contemporary Literary Criticism: Excerpts from Criticism of the Works of Today's Novelists, Poets, Playwrights, Short Story Writers, Scriptwriters, and Other Creative Writers. Detroit: Gale Research. (volume 194 published early 1998) Cumulative indexes included.

Essay and General Literature Index, 1900–1903: An Index to About 40,000 Essays and Articles in 2144 Volumes of Collections of Essays and Miscellaneous Works. Edited by Minnie Earl Sears and Marion Shaw. New York: H. W. Wilson, 1934. (Kept up-to-date with supplements for 1934–1940, 1941–1947, 1948–1954, 1955–1959, 1960–1964, 1965–1969, 1970–1974, 1975–1979, 1980–1984, 1985–1989,1990–1994, annual vols. to date.)

Fiction Catalog. 13th ed. New York: H. W. Wilson, 1996. Supplements, 1996– .

Gordon, Lee and Cheryl Tanaka. *World Historical Fiction Guide for Young Adults.* Fort Atkinson, WI: Highsmith Pr., 1995.

Harner, James L. *Literary Research Guide: A Guide to Reference Sources for the Study of Literatures in English and Related Topics.* 2d ed. New York: Modem Language Association of America, 1993.

Keller, Dean Howard. *Index to Plays in Periodicals.* Rev. and enl. ed. Metuchen, NJ: Scarecrow, 1979.

Klein, Leonard S. *Encyclopedia of World Literature in the 20th* Century. 2nd ed. New York: Frederick Ungar, 1984. (4 vols.) Vol. 5 edited by Walter D. Glanze, 1993.

A well lit area encourages reading.

Kuntz, Joseph Marshall. *Poetry Explication: A Check List of Interpretation Since 1925 of British and American Poems Past and Present.* 3rd ed. Boston: G. K. Hall, 1980.

McGarry, Daniel D., and Sarah Harriman White. *World Historical Fiction Guide: An Annotated Chronological, Geographical and Topical List of Selected Historical Novels.* 2nd ed. Metuchen, NJ: Scarecrow, 1973.

Magill, Frank N. *Masterpieces of World Literature in Digest Form.* New York: Harper, 1952–91.

Masterplots. 2nd revised edition, ed. by Frank Magill. Englewood Cliffs, NJ: Salem Press, 1996. (Available series include: European Fiction, British and Commonwealth Fiction, American Fiction, Short Stories, World Fiction, Women's Literature, Nonfiction, Poetry, Juvenile and Young adult literature, and Drama.)

Masterplots Annual Volume, 1954– . Edited by Frank Magill. New York: Salem, 1955– .

Modern Language Association of America. *MLA International Bibliography of Books and Articles on the Modern Language and Literatures, 192 1— .* Published as a supplement to PMLA Journal).

Moss, Joyce and George Wilson. *Literature and Its Time: Profiles of 300 Notable Literary Works and the Historical Events That Influenced Them.* Detroit: Gale Research, 1997. (5 volumes)

Moulton, Charles Wells. *The Library of Literary Criticism of English and American* Authors. Buffalo, NY: Moulton, 1901–05. Eight vols. Reprinted by Peter Smith, 1959.

Nims, John F. *The Columbia Granger's Index to Poetry.* 10th ed. New York: Columbia University Press, 1993.

Palmer, Alan. *Quotations in History: A Dictionary of Historical Quotations c8OO to Present.* New York: Harper & Row, 1976.

Platt, Suzy. *Respectfully Quoted: A Dictionary of Quotations Requested from Congressional Research Service.* Library of Congress, Washington, DC: GPO, 1992.

Play Index, 1949–1952, 1953–1960, 1961–1967, 1968–1972, 1973–1977, 1978–1982, 1983–1987, 1988–1992, 1993–1997. New York: H. W. Wilson, 1949– .

Poetry Index Annual. Great Neck, NY: Granger, 1982– .

Shields, Ellen F. *Contemporary English Poetry: An Annotated Bibliography of Criticism to 1980.* New York: Garland, 1984.

Short Story Criticism: Excerpts from Criticism of the Works of Short Fiction Writers. Edited by Anna J. Sheets. Detroit: Gale Research, 1988– . (v. 27 published in early 1998.)

Short Story Index. New York: H. W. Wilson, 1953– .

Sutton, Roberta. *Speech Index: An Index to 259 Collections of World Famous Orations and Speeches for Various Occasions.* 4th ed. Metuchen, NJ: Scarecrow, 1966. Supplements 1966–1970 by Sutton and Charity Mitchell (1972); supplement, 1971–1975 by Charity Mitchell (1977); supplement, 1966–1980 by Charity Mitchell (1982).

Teachers & Writers Handbook of Poetry Forms. Edited by Ron Padgett. New York: Teachers & Writers Collaborative, 1987.

Williams, Robert Coleman, ed. A *Concordance to the Collected Poems of Dylan Thomas.* Lincoln: University of Nebraska Press, 1966.

11. Governmental Information and Government Documents

Objectives

After studying this chapter the student shall be able to
- find names and addresses of congressmen and state officials in any district in any state
- find the name, address and organizational history of any federal agency
- find information about function and membership of any congressional committee
- use sources to locate data on local governments
- use the *Congressional Record* to find information on congressional proceedings
- find documents using indexes and bibliographies
- use the *Monthly Catalog* to find specific documents
- recognize the indexes and guides for documents located in the library
- determine the type of information available in indexes and directories of depositories

Governments—Local, State, Federal

This section deals with finding information about municipal, county, state or federal governments and their officials. There are many

Seeking assistance at the reference desk.

directories and guides that provide this kind of information and some examples are described in this chapter. If the library does not have these specific titles it will have similar ones. If the student is unable to locate the texts (check the H and J section in the reference section) then they should ask the librarian for assistance.

The *Municipal Year Book*, published by the International City Management Association, provides a variety of information about cities, including profiles, population statistics, types of government, salaries of employees, services provided and the names of officials (e.g., mayor, police chief and fire chief). It also includes discussions of the state regulations that affect municipalities. The volume has both textual descriptions and comparative charts. A recent publication that will have one volume for each state is titled *(name of state) Facts — Flying the Colors*, published by the same company which publishes *Taylor's Encyclopedia*. This set looks at each state, county by county and includes information concerning the economy, community services, recreation, transportation, county governments, etc. The text includes charts, photographs, population, names of small communities and many statistics. There is an explanation at the beginning of each volume that includes information on the sources used to compile the included data. The set began publication in 1984 and some of the early volumes have already been updated with new editions. Volumes for several additional states are issued each year. Another useful source of information on municipal and county governments is the *County and City Data Book*, which is published by the U.S. Bureau of the Census as a supplement to the *Statistical Abstracts of the United States.*

There are several other sources of information about state governments and elected officials. Many states publish a handbook describing the organization of the state government. For example, New York State publishes the *Manual for the Use of the Legislature of the State of New York* (commonly referred to as the "blue book"). This annual volume provides a copy of the state's constitution, a short history of the state, names of elected officials, biographies and photographs of the highest ranking members of the executive department and state legislature, and a complete organizational description of all departments of state government. These descriptions include names of department heads, office addresses and discussions of each department's responsibilities. They also include some political information, such as the names and addresses of state and county major party officeholders.

Another source of information on elected state and federal officials is *Taylor's Encyclopedia of Governmental Officials, Federal and State.* This encyclopedia includes a large variety of information about government (in easy-to-use format), such as copies of the Constitution, the Declaration of Independence, a list of all former presidents and vice presidents (with pictures of both, when available), cabinet members and their chief aides, all congressional committees including congressional membership, a list (with pictures) of Supreme Court members and former chief justices, and names of all judges in the federal court system (eg., district courts, courts of appeals, claims, etc.). This encyclopedia also includes names, addresses, phone numbers and descriptions of U.S. independent governmental agencies. Information on each state includes a map showing state and federal election districts, with voting patterns (by major political parties), names of elected officials, and state, federal and chief state executives. There are additional charts and descriptions too numerous to include here. This encyclopedia has a new volume every two years and is updated with monthly supplements.

The federal government publishes another item, the *United States Government Manual* (formally the *United States Government Organization Manual*), annually and it is invaluable in untangling the mysteries of locating agencies within particular departments, what their functions are, where they are located (including regional offices) and who is in charge. The manual includes organizational charts that help in determining the hierarchical structure of each agency. The inclusion of regional offices with the names, addresses and phone numbers is also useful. Finally, the manual includes a comprehensive subject index that can be used to decide which agency or agencies are involved with specific tasks.

The Government Printing Office (GPO) issues the *Congressional Directory* that has a brief biography of every member of Congress. Besides the biographies, it includes the district numbers and the counties within each district. Also included are all committee assignments, statistical information about Congress, floor plans of the Capitol building, names of members of the executive branch, diplomats and consular officers in the United States, and members of the press who are entitled to admission to Congress, as well as other esoteric but useful bits of information about Congress. The *Congressional Staff Directory* contains the names of members of Congress, but its most functional feature is the listing of all the staff members who work for members of Congress and on congressional committees. The directory also lists 9,900 cities with a population of more than 1,500 along with the names of members of congress who represent the city. The key personnel aides to the executive branch are recorded with the office addresses, titles and phone numbers.

The *Congressional Quarterly Almanac*, published annually, is particularly valuable in providing information on actions taken by Congress during a particular year. It also encompasses other information such as roll call votes, lobbyists and presidential messages to Congress. The summaries of legislation, background and reports of action taken provide beginning information for researching congressional action in any area.

The *Congressional Record* is issued daily and contains the complete text of presidential messages, debates and congressional speeches. It also contains votes on all bills, although the texts of the bills are not included. The GPO publishes the *Record* only when Congress is in session. Indexes are published after the session ends. Members may add to the *Record* and this additional information, "extension of remarks," may be included as an appendix but may be omitted from the final edition of the *Record*.

The format, order of information and indexing have varied since the *Record* began in 1873, so one should read the introductory remarks before using the *Record* or its indexes. For materials before 1873 the following titles should be consulted: *Debates and Proceedings, Annals of Congress* (1789–1824); *Register of Debates* (1824–1837); and *Congressional Globe* (1833–1873). They are published in both microfilm and paper copy.

Government Documents

Governments at all levels publish many documents. The United States government documents are usually easier to identify and locate than those of small municipalities or county governments. Most state governments publish checklists of their publications which simply identify publications. Libraries designated as "depositories," receive documents free of charge from municipal, county, state or federal governments.

The scope and quality of holdings in a library depend on a variety of factors, such as the date of institution and how heavily the public uses the holdings. Theft, damage and misplacement cause document loss. Some depositories do not receive all documents. These libraries are designated as selective depositories, since they choose only those documents they wish to receive. Libraries have indexes and guides to documents and directories of depository libraries. Federal documents and those reports produced by federal contracts are not copyrighted and the public is free to use them.

Federal Depository Library System

Congress created the federal depository library system by enactment in 1857 and 1858. In 1869 the position of superintendent of documents was created. The Printing Act of 1895 consolidated many previous laws and departments which dealt with aspects of preparation, printing and distribution of public documents. This act also established a "systematic program for bibliographic control" with the creation of *Monthly Catalog* and the *Document Catalog*. This act also expanded the number of depositories and created "by law" depositories which included state libraries, governmental agency libraries and West Point and Annapolis.

This system was relatively unchanged until 1962 when the Depository Act of 1962 was passed.

Figure 11.1 U.S. Monthly Catalog
of Government Publications

forations.]   • Paper, $22.20 (basic manual and supplementary material for an indefinite period) ; add $5.50 for foreign mailing. ● Item 30–A–4   A 101.6/2 : 973/ch.1–8/rep.

00053 Meat and poultry inspection regulations, Change 8. Dec. 8, 1973. [8] p. 4° (Meat and Poultry Inspection Program.) [Issued with perforations.] • Paper, $22.00 (basic and supplementary material for indefinite period) add $5.50 for foreign mailing. ● Item 30–A–4   A 101.6/2 : 973/ch.8

00054 Screwworm. Aug. 1974. 6 p. il. 4° +   A 101.21.Scr 6

ARMS CONTROL AND DISARMAMENT AGENCY
Washington, DC 20451

00055 Arms limitation agreements, July 1974 summit. [July 1974.] 8 p. il. 4° ([Publication 73.]) +   AC 1.2 : Ar 5/5

00056 Documents on disarmament, 1972 [with bibliography ; compiled by Robert W. Lambert and others]. [May 1974.] xviii+959 p. il. ([Publication 69.]) • Paper, $7.50 (S/N 0700–00046). ● Item 865–B
                                                                       AC 1.11/2 : 972

00057 SALT lexicon. [1973.] cover title, [5]+18 p. 4° #   AC 1.2 : Sa 3

00058 Statement by Fred C. Ikle, director, Arms Control and Disarmament Agency, before Subcommittee on National Security Policy and Scientific Developments of the Committee of Foreign Affairs, House of Representatives, Oct. 3, 1974. Oct. 3, 1974 6+[1] p. 4° +   AC 1.12 : Ik 6/2

ARMY DEPARTMENT, Defense Dept.
Washington, DC 20310

AMC pamphlets. (Army Materiel Command.)
00059   706–360. Engineering design handbook : Military vehicle electrical systems [with bibliographies]. June 1974. cover title, [604] p. il. 4° #   ● Item 322–A   D 101.22/3 : 706–360

Army Electronics Command, Fort Monmouth, N.J.: Research and development technical report ECOM (series). (Reports control symbol OSD–1366.)
00060   5512. Design concept of forward area Rawinsonde set (FARS) : by Raymond I. Robbiani. Oct. 1973. cover title, [2]+12+[3] p. il. 4° (Atmospheric Science Laboratory.) [Includes list of atmospheric sciences research papers.] #   D 111.9/4 : 5512
00061   5541. High resolution temperature sonde for lower atmosphere [with list of literature cited] : by Ricardo Pena and H. N. Schwartz. May 1974. cover title, [2]+17+[8] p. il. 4° [DA task IT061102B53A–17.] #
                                                                       D 111.9/4 : 5541

00062 CIF (command information film catalog) 1973 ; prepared by Army Command Information Unit. [1972.] cover title, 102 p. 4° (Office of the Chief of Information.) #   D 101.2 : F 47/973

Field manual FM (series).
00063   3–22. Fallout prediction [with list of references]. Oct. 1973. cover title, 80 p. il. 4° [Issued with perforations. Supersedes TM 3–210, Dec. 3, 1967, including all changes.] # ● Item 324   D 101.20 : 3–22

Pamphlet.
00064   18–11. Management information systems catalog of interim data elements and codes. Mar. 1974. cover title, [345] p. 4° [Issued with perforations.] + ● Item 327 (Rev. 1969)   D 101.22 : 18–11
00065   360–539. See Information for Armed Forces, Office of, DoD pamphlet PA–11A.
00066   550–24. Area handbook for Lebanon [with bibliographies ; by] Harvey H. Smith [and others]. 2d edition. 1974. xlvi+354 p. il. [Prepared by Foreign Area Studies, American University. Supersedes edition of July 1969.] • Cloth, $5.70. ● Item 327 (Rev. 1969)   D 101.22 : 550–24/2 L.C. card 74–13241

@For Sale by National Technical Information Service, Springfield, VA 22151
●Sent to Depository Libraries

Figure 11.2 U.S. Monthly Catalog
of Government Publications

HEALTH AND HUMAN SERVICES
DEPARTMENT
Washington, DC 20201

91-11384

HE 1.2:Se 6/2

Services benefits for older persons : are you eligible? — [Washington, D.C.?] : Dept. of Health and Human Services, [1990] [10] p. ; 21 cm. — (Department of Health and Human Services pub. ; no. 10951) Cover title. Shipping list no.: 90-735-P. "September 1990"—P. [4] of cover. ●Item 445

　　1. Aged — Medical care — United States. 2. Old age assistance — United States. 3. Social security beneficiaries — United States. I. United States. Dept. of Health and Human Services. II. Series: DHHS publication ; no. 10951. OCLC 23095394

SOCIAL SECURITY ADMINISTRATION
Health and Human Services Dept.
Baltimore, MD 21235

91-11385

HE 3.94:990

Fast facts & figures about social security. [Washington, D.C.] : U.S. Dept. of Health and Human Services, Social Security Administration, Office of Policy, Office of Research & Statistics : Supt. of Docs., U.S. G.P.O., [1986?- Supt. of Docs., U.S. Govt. Print. Off., Washington, DC 20402-9325

　　v. : col. ill. ; 22 cm. (SSA publication ; no. 13-11785)

　　Annual

　　$2.25

　　[1986]- Shipping list no.: 91-061-P. 1990. ●Item 516 S/N 017-070-00450-4 @ GPO

　　⸍1. Social security — United States — Statistics — Periodicals. I. United States. Social Security Administration. Office of Research and Statistics. II. Series. HD7123.F37 89-644320 368.4/3/00973021 /20 OCLC 20667525

There are 53 regional depositories which receive all items designated for depositories. Each state has a regional depository and some state have two regional depositories. There are over 1,350 selective depositories. Each congressional district is entitled to have two depositories although with changes in district boundaries over the years some districts have more than two. Executive departments of the federal government, accredited law schools, service academies and independent government agencies can request to be depositories.

Depository libraries are subject to rules concerning free access to the collection by the general public, the retaining and discarding of documents and inspection of the collection by staff from the superintendent of documents office.

Some depository items are published only in paper format, others only in microform or magnetic format and others are available in either paper or microform format (in which case the depository library can choose which format it prefers).

SuDoc Classification System

Government documents are not harder to use or find, they are just organized differently. Unlike the Dewey Decimal or Library of Congress classification systems which arrange materials by subject, the SuDoc system is a provenance (or hierarchy) system. This system arranges material by the issuing agency and its various departments. The documents are arranged in a hierarchy order for each agency. They are specified as follows: parent agency, subagency, series or generic type, individual publication and date. See Figure 11.1 and 11.2 from the *Monthly Catalog* and note that the departments names are in the center of the column. The SuDoc number is also in heavy black type. It begins with one or two letters to identify the agency (see Figure 11.2). The HE is for the Health and Human Services Agency. The number after the letter(s) and before the decimal indicate the level, e.g. 1 for cabinet level document. The number after the decimal indicates the type of document, e.g. directive, report, newsletter, etc. As with the Dewey and LC systems there are charts noting the numbers used for departmental levels and types of documents. The numbers and letter after the colon provide information about the update of publication and the format of the document, e.g. 990 means published in 1990. Formats can be paper, microform, magnetic tape, etc. Each format has a specific number. The frequent reorganization within the federal government sometimes causes disorder with this system.

The Monthly Catalog is also available via OCLC's FirstSearch. Figure 11.3 shows a title located by searching for tornado warnings. Tags in the margin help identify author, title, imprint information and also includes added authors, notes, assigned subject headings, collation information *Monthly Catalog* number (MOCATNO:) and OCLC number.

Figure 11.3 OCLC Screen
GPO Monthly Catalog

INNOPAC Z39.50 searching GPO at FirstSearch Databases
You searched for the WORD: tornado warning

Record #1 of 7

AUTHOR   United States.
TITLE   NEXRAD, tornado warnings, and National Weather
        modernization : hearing before the Subcommittee on Space
        of the Committee on Science, Space, and Technology, U.S.
        House of Representatives, One Hundred Third Congress,
        Second session, July 29, 1994.
IMPRINT   Washington : U.S. G.P.O. : For sale by the U.S. G.P.O.,
        Supt. of Docs., Congressional Sales Office, 1994
NOTE   Distributed to some depository libraries in microfiche.
        Shipping list no.: 95-0012-P. "No. 151." Includes
        bibliographical references.
        English
SUBJECT   United States. National Weather Service.
        Meteorological stations, Radar United States.
        Meteorological stations United States.
        Tornado warning systems United States.
        Weather forecasting United States.
ADD AUTHOR Congress.
        House.
        Committee on Science, Space, and Technology.
        Subcommittee on Space.
APPEARS IN 0160463890
LOCAL INFO PUB TYPE: Book
        FORMAT: iii, 375 p. : ill., maps ; 24 cm.
        ITEM NO: 1025-A-01 1025-A-02 (MF)
        MOCAT NO: 95062682
        OCLC NO: 31877120

Government Printing Office (GPO)

The Printing Act of 1860 created the GPO and it opened on March 4, 1861. The GPO is officially an agency of the legislative branch but the president appoints the public printer with the consent of Congress. The public printer and the GPO are accountable to that body. The office of superintendent of documents was established on March 3, 1869, as a part of the Department of the Interior and transferred to the GPO in 1895. The Congressional Joint Committee on Printing (JCP) is a sort of board of directors for the GPO.

Figure 11.4 OCLC Screen FirstSearch

INNOPAC Z39.50 searching ERIC at FirstSearch Databases
You searched for the SUBJECT: phonics whole language kindergarten
                                    Record #1 of 6
AUTHOR   Ball, Eileen Wynne
TITLE   Phonological Awareness: Implications for Whole Language
           and Emergent Literacy Programs.
NOTE   PUB TYPE: Journal article Research/technical report
           Reviews the relationship between phonological awareness
           and early reading. Follow-up data from a group of 38
           first-grade children who had low letter-sound knowledge
           in kindergarten found that those who received
           phonological awareness intervention in kindergarten
           performed better than their first-grade peers on word
           recognition and reading decoding measures. (Author/CR)
           English
           Topics in Language Disorders v17 n3 p14-26 May 1997
SUBJECT   Decoding (Reading) ericd
           Intervention ericd
           Phoneme Grapheme Correspondence ericd
           Phonics ericd
           Reading Difficulties ericd
           Word Recognition ericd
           Beginning Reading ericd
           Followup Studies ericd
           Kindergarten Children ericd
           Oral Language ericd
           Program Effectiveness ericd
           Whole Language Approach ericd

The GPO is the largest publisher in the United States and perhaps in the world. It acts like other publishers and also prints many items. Due to the large volume of material to be printed, the GPO contracts out many of the printing jobs to small printing companies. It coordinates the operations from the Washington, D.C. offices. There are also 13 regional printing offices as well as the Consumer Information Office in Pueblo, Colorado, which acts as a distributor. The GPO also operates some bookstores which sell government documents. Some bookstore chains also stock some government documents.

The 1895 law allows the superintendent of documents to sell documents and the GPO selects titles to include in the sales program. Currently there is a formula for determining the sale price: cost + 50 percent. This sales program generates revenue for the GPO and allows the agency to support the documents sent free to depository libraries and those documents distributed to the general public free of charge (many through the center in Pueblo). Recently the GPO made some changes in its system of payment and now accepts major credit cards besides pre-payment and deposit accounts. The GPO sells many documents to commercial publishers which then may be reprinted and sold or used in other ways. For example, the census material, in magnetic format, is sold to many types of corporations that can manipulate the data for their own use. All these sales operations generate revenue that makes the GPO a self-sustaining operation, requiring little or no taxpayer funds. Due to cutbacks in the Reagan administration, fewer documents (titles) were published and print runs were smaller thus curtailing the public's access to some information.

Government Printing Office on the Internet

GPO Access is the free electronic access service provided by the Government Printing Office at http://www.access.gpo.gov/su-docs/. All information that is provided through this site is the official published version and can be used without restriction unless specifically noted. Service categories include: government information databases for on-line use; individual Federal agency files available for downloading; collections of government information available for downloading; collections of government information available for free use at a library near you; and user support.

Among the free Federal databases available are: the Federal Register; the Code of Federal Regulations; the Congressional Record; Congressional bills; Commerce Business Daily (CBDNet); Catalog of U.S. Government Publications (MOCAT); the Sales Product Catalog (SPC) and the Government Information Locator Service (GLIS).

Over 4,500 individual Federal agency files are available for free download from the Federal Bulletin Board (FBB). This allows individual agencies to provide to the public free, immediate, and self-service access to Federal information in electronic form. Agencies add files directly to the FBB to insure the latest official information is available.

The Sales Product Catalog (SPC) lists documents available for purchase from the Superintendent of Documents. Orders can be placed on-line, or print out an order form to mail or fax to GPO for processing. The GILS can identify sources of publicly available Federal information sources. This includes both electronic and non-electronic sources. All GILS sources can be searched at the same time.

GPO Access provides an indexed search of more than 1,300 official Federal agencies and military Internet sites. The GPO Access will also locate the federal Depository libraries in your area.

To search GPO Access use wwwaccess.gpo.gov. User support is available Monday-Friday from 7 A.M. to 5 P.M. Eastern time or by phone (1-888-293-6498) or by FAX at 1-202-512-1262. This comprehensive service is funded by the Federal Depository Program (Public Law 10340 the Government Printing Office Electronic Information Enhancement Act, 1993).

National Technical Information Service (NTIS)

The NTIS in the Commerce Department was established on September 2, 1970. Its general purpose is to simplify and improve access to data files of scientific literature, technical reports, etc., from federal agencies and federal contractors. Much of the material available from NTIS may not be available from depository libraries. Not all unclassified documents are designated as depository items. The NTIS is a distributor of some government documents and reports, etc., of research done on government contracts (not considered to be government documents). These materials are in various formats: paper copy, microform, magnetic and CD. The NTIS is required by law to recover its costs from the sale of its documents so it is more expensive to purchase from NTIS than from the GPO. Sometimes, especially with reports of research done on government contracts, documents are available sooner from NTIS than from the GPO. Some of the reports available from NTIS are prepared and published by individuals, corporations, universities, etc., that have done research using federal funds.

The *Government Reports Announcements and Index* (GRA&I) is the main bibliographic tool used to locate and identify material at NTIS. NTIS publishes GRA&I twice monthly with annual accumulations. Its indexes include keyword, personal author, corporate author and contract/grant number. Information for ordering, including codes, prices, format, etc., is also included.

Federal Documents

Most documents sought by library users are United States government publications. The federal documents, most of which are published by the GPO, are indexed and identified in several publications. One can identify early dated documents by using a *Descriptive Catalogue of Government Publications of the United States, September 5, 1774–March 4, 1881*, compiled by Perley Poore, 1885. The *Comprehensive Index to Publications of the United States, 1881–1894* by John G. Ames, 1905, identifies documents in the years following. The current index, *Monthly Catalog of Government Publications* (*Monthly Cat* for short) first appeared in 1895 and is still published monthly. Collections also contain specific checklists and catalogs of federal documents that deal with subjects such as forestry or are records of agencies or departments, such as congressional hearings.

Before using the *Monthly Cat*, one should examine the instructions at the beginning of the volume because the format and indexing have changed from time to time. Each monthly issue is arranged alphabetically by agency issuing the document. Each document is given a number similar to an abstract number, called the *Monthly Cat* number. This number appears in the left margin for each document or column of each page. Early volumes of the *Monthly Cat* had only an annual subject index, but since 1975 additional indexes such as title and report indexes have been added. This makes it easier to identify documents (see figures 11.1 and 11.1). Note the *Monthly Cat* number in the left margin. After the end of the entry in the right hand margin is another indicator, usually a combination of letters and numbers. This is the "SuDoc" number, assigned by the superintendent of documents who is in charge of the GPO and other government printing operations. Depository libraries usually do not catalog their documents but file them by the SuDoc number, which in a sense is the "call" number. The other symbols in the entry show additional information such as where to purchase a copy of the document and its depository status.

Figure 11.2 illustrates the latest format used in the *Monthly Cat*. The *Monthly Cat* number still appears at the left of each entry but the SuDoc number appears in bold at the beginning of each entry. The entries are in the format of the catalog card and each entry still contains information about its depository status. The large black dot shows depository items. The last line of each entry is an OCLC number. The OCLC system will be discussed in Chapter 14. Since 1976 when the *Monthly Cat* changed its format it has been available on magnetic tape. Some large libraries that also have large depository collections like the New York State Library have loaded the tape for the monthly catalog into their On-Line Public Catalog (OPAC). This ensures that users have access to all the information in the *Monthly Cat* since 1976 by using the OPAC only. Easier access to government documents is thus made possible as well as making more individuals aware of the variety of information available from documents. Since documents are not usually in the catalog, many students and faculty forget that they are a valuable source of information. The *Monthly Cat* is also available in some libraries on CDs and via FirstSearch (see Figure 11.3), adding ways of searching for documents.

The *Index to U.S. Government Periodicals* is published commercially and is an index to 185 selected periodicals published by the U.S. government. The index is published quarterly with annual accumulations. Its format is similar to that used by the Wilson indexes discussed in Chapter 8.

The Congressional Information Services (CIS) publishes a variety of reference books about government and indexes to documents, including the *American Statistics Index*, *CIS/Index* and *CIS Serials Set Index*. CIS publications all include lengthy explanations and examples of entries and this introductory material should be read before the student uses any CIS publication for the first time. As its title suggests, *American Statistics Index* presents statistics published by the federal government. Many departments and agencies besides the Census Bureau publish statistics. The *CIS/Index* has several sections: Legislative Histories of U.S. Public Laws, Index to Congressional Publications and Public Laws, and Abstracts of Congressional Publications. This index is published monthly with an annual accumulation, the *CIS/Annual*. Multi-year indexes are available for the index volumes, but not the abstract volumes. The *U.S. Serial Set* has been known by various names and has changed in format and content. Generally the set consists of congressional publications; reports and documents of both house and senate, treaty documents and senate executive reports. This set is a primary source for locating the texts of reports, treaties, bill, special reports, etc. The numbering system in the *U.S. Serial Set* has changed from time to time so it is important to consult the introductory material. Since 1970 CIS has provided full-text microfiche for all publications covered in CIS indexes. Many libraries (not necessarily depositories) have purchased these microfiche. CIS uses its own numbering system for its microfiche

Figure 11.5 Resources in Education

ED 323 901   HE 023 913
Broome, Benjamin J. And Others
Long-Range Planning in a University Setting: A
  Case Study.
Pub Date—Nov 89
Note—38p.; Paper presented at the Annual Meet-
  ing of the Speech Communication Association
  (75th, San Francisco, CA, November 18-21,
  1989).
Pub Type— Speeches/Meeting Papers (150) — Re-
  ports - Evaluative (142)
EDRS Price - MF01/PC02 Plus Postage.
Descriptors—Case Studies. *College Planning, De-
  partments, Higher Education, *Long Range Plan-
  ning,   *Mission   Statements,   Models,
  *Organizational Objectives, Policy Formation,
  Speech Communication
Identifiers—*George Mason University VA, Organizational Research, *Strategic Planning
  A case study is presented that used the methods
of Generic Design Science to conduct strategic
planning for the Department of Communication at
George Mason University, Fairfax, Virginia. Applied in the context of an academic environment,
the methods yielded a comprehensive management
and planning design for focusing administration and
faculty efforts over a 3-year period. The products of
the design work include: (1) an intent structure of
objectives; (2) alternative options for accomplishing
the objectives; (3) a 3-year departmental plan; and
(4) a mission statement. In the judgment of the departmental chair, the approach has been of benefit
to the department in establishing a standard for continuous planning and design. Equally important, the
faculty has identified priorities to guide the development of curriculum, research, and allocation of resources. A mission statement, the structural model,
and an options profile are included. Contains nine
references. (Author/GLR)

edition of the *U.S. Serial Set* and those numbers will also appear in the CIS indexes.

There are other indexes to documents that are subject specific and often prepared by specific agencies, for example, *Scientific and Technical Aerospace Reports* (STAR) produced at NASA.

Educational Resources Information Center (ERIC)

The collecting, abstracting, indexing, distribution, etc., of signifi-cant education related reports and journal articles is the mission of ERIC, the national system of clearinghouses located at universities and or pro-fessional organizations. *Resources in Education* (RIE) (see Figure 11.5), a GPO publication, is an abstracting journal providing bibliographic information and identification of the reports, published and unpub-

Figure 11.6 Thesaurus of ERIC Descriptors

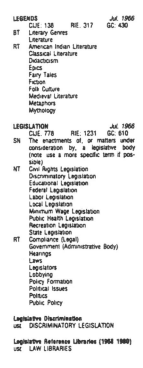

lished. Libraries may subscribe to ERIC and receive copies of the reports in microfiche format. The fiche are usually filed by the number found at the beginning of each entry in RIE (see Figure 11.5) the ERIC document number. The numbering system is similar to but not identical to the system used in the *Monthly Cat.* Each entry includes general bibliographical information and an abstract the same as other abstracting sources discussed in Chapter 8. The entries also contain other information such as contract numbers, where to get paper copies and their cost, descriptors (useful for searching ERIC on-line for related items), etc. ERIC is also available via FirstSearch (see Figure 11.4).

Current Index to Journals in Education published by Oryx Press is the second index providing access to materials collected by ERIC. This publication indexes approximately 750 journals/serials, and issues monthly and semi-annual accumulations. The information included in each entry is typical of other abstracting services discussed in Chapter 8 with the addition of a list of descriptors.

Students also may identify ERIC documents by searching the

indexes via on-line vendors, such as DIALOG, or on CDs available in many libraries. To help in searching the ERIC files on-line or via CDs it is useful to consult the *Thesaurus of ERIC Descriptors* (Figure 11.6).

Exercises for Chapter 11

1. Using the catalog, list the indexes and guides to documents in your library. Record call numbers for future reference.
2. Using the *Monthly Catalog*, answer the following questions.
   (A) Check the subject index for 1980, 1985 and 1995 for documents issued each year on Biological Warfare.
      1. Compare the number of documents issued each year.
      2. What agency issued the most documents?
      3. Are most of the documents found in depository libraries?
   (B) Locate and identify the documents dealing with the Whitewater investigation.
3. Choose one U.S. senator from your home state and locate the following information:
   (A) Washington address
   (B) committee assignments
   (C) names of chief aides
4. Find the following information:
   (A) The name of the vice president under Harry Truman.
   (B) The location of the Federal Reserve Banks.
   (C) The name of the chief judge in your state.
5. Find the population of your home county. List all the sources in your library which provide this information. You should include all sources discussed in previous chapters.

Important Terms in Chapter 11

Monthly Catalog number	*depository library*
SuDoc number	*GPO*
Superintendent of Documents	*municipality*
NTIS	*ERIC*
CIS	

Important Books for Chapter 11

GUIDES

Clark, Carol Lea. *A Citizen's Directory: Who to Contact to Get Things Done.* New York: Facts on File, 1983.

Directory of Government Document Collections and Librarians 7th ed. Government Documents Roundtable, American Library Association, ed. by Barbara Kile and Audrey Taylor. Washington, DC: Congressional Information Service, 1997.

Garner, Diane L. *The Complete Guide to Citing Government Documents: A Manual for Writers and Librarians.* Rev. ed. Government Documents Roundtable, American Library Association. Washington, DC: Congressional Information Services, 1993.

Government Reference Books. Edited by LeRoy Schwarzkopf. Littleton, CO: Libraries Unlimited, 1970-. (Biennial guide to U.S. government publications.)

Hardy, Gayle J. and Judith Schiek Robinson. *Subject Guide to U.S. Government Reference Sources.* 2nd ed. Englewood, CO: Libraries Unlimited, 1996.

Herman, Edward. *Locating United States Government Information: a guide to sources.* Buffalo, NY: W. S. Hein, 1997. Also available is an Internet supplement.

Hoffmann, Frank W. *Guide to Popular U.S. Government Publications.* 4th ed. Englewood, CO: Libraries Unlimited, 1997.

Houston, James E. ed. *Thesaurus of ERIC Descriptors.* 13th ed., Phoenix, AZ: Oryx, 1995.

Kelly, Melody S. *Using Government Documents: A How-to-Do-It Manual for School Librarians.* New York: Neal-Schuman Publishers, 1992.

Maxwell, Bruce. *Washington Online: How to Access the Federal Government on the Internet* 1998. Washington, DC: Congressional Quarterly, 1997.

Mayros, Van, and Michael D. Wemer. *Guide to Information from Government Sources.* Radnor, PA: Chilton Books, 1983.

Morehead, Joe. *Introduction to United States Public Documents.* 5th ed. Littleton, CO: Libraries Unlimited, 1996.

Municipal Government Reference Sources: Publications and Collections. Edited for the American Association Government Roundtable by Peter Hernon. New York: R. R. Bowker, 1978.

Notess, Greg R. *Government Information on the Internet.* Lanham, MD: Bernan Press, 1997.

Parish, David. *State Government Reference Publications,* 2nd ed. Littleton, CO: Libraries Unlimited, 1981.

Pokorny, Elizabeth J. *U.S. Government Documents: A Practical Guide for NonProfessionals in Academic and Public Libraries.* Englewood, CO: Libraries Unlimited, 1989.

Ross, John M. *How to Use Major Indexes to U.S. Government Publications.* Chicago, IL: American Library Association, 1989.

Wilcox, Jerome Kear. *Manual on the Use of state Publications.* Chicago: American Library Association, 1940.

U.S. Publications—Indexes

American Statistics Index. V. 1-, 1973- Washington, DC: Congressional Information Service, 1973- .

Ames, John G. *Comprehensive Index to the Publications of the United States Government, 1881–1893.* Washington, DC: GOP, 1976.

CIS/Index. V. 1– , 1970– . Bethesda, MD: Congressional Information Service, 1970– .

Congressional Record: Containing the Proceedings and Debates of the 43 Congress— March 4, 1987– . Washington, DC: GOP, 1973– . V. 1– . (Issues daily while Congress is in session. Revised, bound form issued at the end of each session.)

Current Index to Journals in Education. Phoenix, AZ: Oryx, 1969– .

Government Reports Announcements & Index. V. 75– , 1975– . Springfield, VA: U.S. Department of Commerce, NTIS, 1975– . Earlier volumes have various titles.

Index to Annals of the Congress of the United States, 1st Congress Through 18th Congress, 1789–1824. Washington, DC: U.S. Historical Documents Institution, 1970 (reprint ed.).

Index to the Register of Debates in Congress. Containing Indexes to the Appendices, 18th Congress, 1st Session, 1824–1837. Washington, DC: Gales & Seaton, 1976. Compiled from authentic materials (reprint ed.).

Index to U.S. Government Periodicals, 1970– . Chicago: Infodata International, 1970– .

Indexes to the Congressional Globe, 23rd Congress to the 42nd Congress, Dec. 2, 1833–March 3, 1873. Washington, DC: Office of the Congressional Globe, 1970. (Reprint of 1834–73 ed.)

Poore, Benjamin Perley. *A Descriptive Catalogue of the Government*

Publications of the United States, Sept. 5, 1774–March 4, 1881. Comp. by order of Congress. Washington, D.C.: GOP, 1885.

Resources in Education. Phoenix, AZ: Oryx, 1980– .

Scientific & Technical Aerospace Reports. National Aeronautics & Space Administration. *STAR, and Abstract Journal*. V. 1– , 1963– . Washington, D.C.: GOP, 1963– .

United Nations Publication

Brimmer, Brenda, et al. *A Guide to the Use of the United Nations Documents*. Dobbs Ferry, NY: Oceana, 1962.

A Comprehensive Handbook of the United Nations: A Documentary Presentation in Two Volumes. Compiled and edited by Minchuan Ku. New York: Monarch Press, 1978.

McConaughy, John Bothwell, and Hazel Janet Blanks. *A Student's Guide to United Nations Documents and Their Use*. New York: Council on International Relations and United Nations Affairs, 1969.

United Nations and Dag Hammerskjold Library. *Checklist of United Nationals Documents, 1946–1949*. New York, 1949–1953.

_____ and _____. *United Nations Documents Index*. New York, pub. Monthly beginning with 1950.

_____ and _____. Secretary-General. *Public Papers of the Secretaries-General of the United Nations*. Andrew W. Cordier, Wilder Foote, and Max Harrelson, eds. New York: Columbia University Press, 1969–1977 (8 vols.).

UN Secretary-General: A Bibliography. New York: United Nationals. Dag Hammarskjold Library, 1996. Access via World Wide Web. "This bibliography is a comprehensive listing of books and journal articles concerning in whole, or in part, with the office and powers of the secretary-general of the United Nations..." (Preface).

Winton, Harry N. M., comp. *Publications of the United Nations System: A Reference Guide*. New York: R. R. Bowker, 1972.

Guides to Government and Elected Officials

Congressional Quarterly Almanac, a Service for Editors and Commentators. V. 1– , 1945– . Washington, D.C.: Congressional Quarterly, 1945– .

Congressional Staff Directory, 1959– . Indianapolis: Bobbs-Merrill, 1959– .

Municipal Year Book: An Authoritative Resume of Activities and Statistical Data of American Cities. Washington, D.C.: International City Management Association, 1934– .

New York Department of State. *Manual for the Use of the Legislature of the State of New York, 1840– .* Albany, 1840– .

Official Congressional Directory. Washington, D.C.: GOP, 1900– .

State Blue Books, Legislative Manuals and Reference Publications: A Selective Bibliography. Edited by Lynn Hellebust. Topeka, KS: Government Research Service, 1990.

Taylor's Encyclopedia of Government Officials, Federal and States. V. 1– , 1967– . Dallas: Political Research, 1967/68– .

United States Bureau of the Census. *County and City Data Book.* 1949– . Washington, D.C.: GOP, 1949– .

United States Manual 1973– . Federal Register, Washington, D.C.: GOP, 1973– . (Earlier title, United States Government Organization Manual.)

12. Biography

Objectives

After studying this chapter the student shall be able to
 • list the biographical sources the library holds
 • figure out what each source contains
 • locate biographical information for specific individuals
 • use the Internet and on-line sources to locate biographical information

General Information

Students often think of biographies as book-length histories of individuals, but there are many sources that provide brief biographical information. Often the only bit of information needed is a current address, date of birth, place of employment or current occupation. To find the sources of biography in the library, one checks the catalog under the subject Biography. There is an extensive list of entries under the broad heading Biography and entries with subheadings such as Biography — Dictionaries. The student should take a brief cursory look through all the entries. To find a book-length biography of a specific person, look in the catalog under the individual's name as a subject, e.g., Lincoln, Abraham. Those which are subject entries refer to books with biographical information. When looking through the entries under the subject heading Biography one will find some biographical indexes, some for biographical dictionaries and some for biographical encyclopedias.

Figure 12.1 Biography Index

Figure 12.2 Search of
Biography Index via OCLC's FirstSearch

INNOPAC Z39.50 searching Biography Index at FirstSearch Databases
  You searched for the SUBJECT: teresa
  183 entries found, entries 1-8
Teresa, Mother, 1910-1997, Yugoslav nun and missionary.
  1 Mother Teresa.
  2 Saint of the streets.
  3 Death of a 'saint'.
  4 Mother Teresa, R.I.P.
  5 'Blessed are the merciful': Mother Teresa (1910-1997).
  6 Mother Teresa, hope of the despairing, dies at 87.
Urrea, Teresa, 1873-1906, Mexican mystic and healer.
  7 Notable Latino Americans : a biographical dictionary / (by) Matt S.
Teresa, Mother, 1910-1997, Yugoslav nun and missionary.
  8 (Obituary).

Each of these sources includes many individuals. A few examples of biographical sources available in many libraries are listed below.

Indexes

Biography Index, (Figure 12.1) published by H. W. Wilson Company, is a quarterly index to biographical information in books and periodicals. Multi-year volumes replace quarterly and annual volumes. They are arranged alphabetically by the name of the biographee, and at the back of the volume is a list of the biographees arranged by profession and occupation. The format on the print index is the same as other Wilson indexes discussed in earlier chapters. In Figure 12.1 find the entries for Mother Teresa. Figure 12.2 is a search of *Biography Index* via OCLC's FirstSearch for entries about Mother Teresa. Note that the whole database for *Biography Index* contains 183 entries and a summary of the first 8 found is listed. To find complete information on each of those entries it is necessary to follow screen directions (not reproduced here). Figure 12.3 is another search of *Biography Index* via FirstSearch. This time an author search has been done for the book by Claire Jordan Mohan found in the print copy of *Biography Index*. You will notice that the on-line entry provides additional information such as the subject headings assigned to this book.

Figure 12.3 Search of
Biography Index via OCLC's FirstSearch

INNOPAC Z39.50 searching Biography Index at FirstSearch Databases
You searched for the AUTHOR: mohan, clair jordan
Record #1 of 1

AUTHOR   Mohan, Claire Jordan.
     Robbins, Jane,
     il.
TITLE   The young life of Mother Teresa of Calcutta /
     illustrations, Jane Robbins.
IMPRINT   United States Young Sparrow Press, 1996
NOTE   64 p. : bibl il map.
SUBJECT   Teresa, Mother, 1910-1997, Yugoslav nun and missionary
     Juvenile literature.
     Missionaries.
     Nobel prize winners.
     Nuns.
LOCAL INFO FICTION IND.: Nonfiction
     INT. LEVEL: Juvenile
     RECORD TYPE: mon

The *Biography and Genealogy Master Index* is an index to biographies in more than 250 biographical dictionaries and Who's Whos. The base set was published in 1981 and there are five-year cumulations, for 1981 to 1985, 1986 to 1990, 1991–1995, plus annual volumes. This set was preceded by the *Biographical Dictionaries Master Index* published in 1975 and 1976. This set of indexes saves time and eliminates guessing which biographical dictionaries should be consulted.

Marquis Publications

Most of the biographical dictionaries with a title beginning with "Who's Who in…" are published by Marquis. They publish an index to all their biographical publications, *Marquis Who's Who Publications, Index to Who's Who Book*. The 1990 edition includes over 253,500 individuals listed in the latest edition of 13 different Who's Who titles. Not all books in the Who's Who series are published annually. Perhaps the most familiar in the Who's Who series is *Who's Who in America* (Figure 12.4). The volumes in this series include brief biographical information about notable living Americans. Other Marquis Who's Who volumes are

Figure 12.4   Who's Who in America

LACHEMANN, RENE GEORGE, professional sports manager; b. L.A., May 4, 1945. Attended, U. So. Calif. Minor league baseball player, 1964-72; with major league teams Kansas City, 1965-66, Oakland, 1968; minor league baseball team mgr., 1973-81; major league baseball team mgr. Seattle Mariners, 1981-83, Milw. Brewers, 1984; coach Boston Red Sox, 1984-86, Oakland Athletics, 1986-92; mgr. Fla. Marlins, 1993—. Named Southern League Mgr. of Yr., 1976. Office: Fla Marlins 2269 NW 199th St Miami FL 33056*

LACHENBRUCH, ARTHUR HEROLD, geophysicist; b. New Rochelle, N.Y., Dec. 7, 1925; s. Milton Cleveland and Leah (Herold) L.; m. Edith Bennett, Sept. 7, 1950; children: Roger, Charles, Barbara. BA, Johns Hopkins U., 1950; MA, Harvard U., 1954, PhD, 1958. Registered geophysicist and geologist, Calif. Research geophysicist U.S. Geol. Survey, 1951—; vis. prof. Dartmouth Coll., 1963; mem. numerous adv. coms. and panels. Contbr. articles to sci. jours. Mem. Los Altos Hills (Calif.) Planning Commn., 1966-86. Served with USAAF, 1943-46. Recipient Spl. Act award U.S. Geol. Survey, 1970, Meritorious Service award, 1972, Disting. Service award U.S. Dept. Interior, 1978. Fellow AAAS, Am. Geophys. Union (Walter H. Bucher medal 1989), Royal Astron. Soc., Geol. Soc. Am. (Kirk Bryan award 1963), Arctic Inst. N.Am.; mem. Nat. Acad. Sci. Current work: solid-earth geophysics, terrestial heat flow, tectonophysics, permafrost; subspecialties: tectonics, geophysics. Office: US Geol Survey 345 Middlefield Rd Menlo Park CA 94025-3591

LACHENBRUCH, DAVID, editor, writer; b. New Rochelle, N.Y., Feb. 11, 1921; s. Milton Cleveland and Leah Judith (Herold) L.; m. Gladys Kidwell, Dec. 12, 1941; 1 child, Ann Leah Lachenbruch Zulawski. BA, U. Mich., 1942. Corr. Variety, also Detroit Times, 1940-42; reporter, asst. city editor, then wire editor Gazette & Daily, York, Pa., 1946-50; assoc. editor TV Digest with Consumer Electronics, Washington, 1950-58; mng. editor TV Digest with Consumer Electronics, 1959-68; editorial dir. TV Digest with Consumer Electronics, N.Y.C., 1968—; v.p. Warren Pub., Inc., Washington, 1962—. Columnist Electronics Now mag., Video mag.; co-author: The Complete Book of Adult Toys, 1983; contbr. articles to consumer mags.; contbg. editor: N.Y. Times Ency. of TV; author: Videocassette Recorders—The Complete Home Guide, 1978, A Look Inside Television, 1985; cons. Acad. Am. Ency. Served with AUS, 1942-45. Mem. White House Corrs. Assn., Union Internat. de la Presse Electronique. Home: 77 7th Ave New York NY 10011-6644 also: 20 Cross Brook Rd Roxbury CT 06783 Office: 475 Fifth Ave New York NY 10017-6220

LACHEY, JAMES MICHAEL, professional football player; b. St. Henry, Ohio, June 4, 1963. B in Mktg., Ohio State, 1985. With San Diego Chargers, 1985-87, L.A. Raiders, 1988; offensive tackle Washington Redskins, 1988—. Played in Pro Bowl, 1987, 90-91. Office: Washington Redskins PO Box 17247 Dulles Internat Airport Washington DC 20041

LACHMAN, LAWRENCE, business consultant, former department store executive; b. N.Y.C., Jan. 9, 1916; s. Charles and Dorothy (Rubin) L.; m. Judith Lehman, Apr. 8, 1945; children: Robert Ian, Charles Scott. BS summa cum laude, NYU, 1936. Controller James McCreery & Co., N.Y.C., 1938-46; treas., dir. Citizens Utilities Co., Stamford, Conn., 1946-47; treas. Bloomingdale's, N.Y.C., 1947-53; v.p. personnel and ops. Bloomingdale's, 1953-58, exec. v.p. adminstrn. and personnel, 1958-64, pres., chief exec. officer, 1964-69, chmn. bd., chief exec. officer, 1969-78; chmn. bd., chief exec. officer Bus. Mktg. Corp., 1978-80; bd. dirs. DFS Group Ltd., ADVO, Inc. Trustee NYU, 1974-90. Served to maj. USAAF, 1942-46. Decorated Bronze Star; French Legion of Honor; recipient Madden award N.Y. U., 1969. Home: 104 E 68th St Apt 5A New York NY 10021-5905

Figure 12.5 Contemporary Authors

BUETTNER, Dan 1960-

PERSONAL: Born in 1960.

ADDRESSES: Office—c/o MayaQuest, 529 South Seventh St., Suite 507, Minneapolis, MN 55415. *E-mail*—dbuettner@usinternet.com.

CAREER: Explorer, journalist, and photographer. AfricaTrek (bicycle tour), leader, 1992-93; MayaQuest (series of interactive expeditions), leader, 1995, 1996, 1997; participant in other record-setting bicycle expeditions, including Americastrek, 1986-87, and Sovietrek, 1990; guest on radio and television programs, including *National Geographic Explorer, Late Night with David Letterman,* and *Prime Time Live.*

AWARDS, HONORS: Minnesota Book Award, 1995, for *Sovietrek;* Emmy Award, American Academy of Television Arts and Sciences, 1995, for a documentary program about Africatrek; three Guinness World Records; named "Athlete of the Week," *NBC Today.*

WRITINGS:

(Author and photographer) *Sovietrek: A Journey by Bicycle across Russia,* Lerner Publications (Minneapolis, MN), 1994.
MayaQuest: The Interactive Expedition, with photographs by Doug Mason, Onion Press, 1996.
Africatrek, Lerner Publications, 1996.

Also author of *Inside Grand Bahama.*

SIDELIGHTS: Cyclist, photographer, and author Buettner has sought adventure across five continents. His record as the premier long-distance cyclist in the world has brought him to the attention of national television and radio audiences, as well as readers of such well-known periodicals as *Sports Illustrated, Bicycling, Outside,* and the *Chicago Tribune.* Among his many outstanding accomplishments is his success in linking thousands of schools and on-line subscribers to some of the world's foremost archaeologists working in Central America through satellite communication and the Internet. His AfricaTrek in 1992-93 demonstrated racial cooperation as he led a team of two black and two white cyclists across Africa. Through his lectures and writings, he has challenged young people and adults to take risks, set goals, and realize their dreams.

Sue A. Norkeliunas, in a review of *Sovietrek* for *School Library Journal,* praised not only Buettner's writing as "highly readable," but also noted his "excellent" full-color photographs which enhance the text and "lend a personal touch to the descriptions." According to Roger Sutton of the *Bulletin of the Center for Children's Books,* Buettner's "style is livelier than *National Geographic . . .* and there's a good sense of the grind that such a journey can be."

BIOGRAPHICAL/CRITICAL SOURCES:

PERIODICALS

Bulletin of the Center for Children's Books, November, 1994, pp. 81-82.
Horn Book Guide, spring, 1995, p. 159.
Kirkus Reviews, July 15, 1994, p. 979.
Library Journal, June 1, 1996, p. 134; August, 1996, p. 97.
School Library Journal, September, 1994, p. 225.

*   *   *

BUFFIE, Margaret 1945-

PERSONAL: Born March 29, 1945, in Winnipeg, Manitoba, Canada; daughter of Ernest William John (a lithographer) and Evelyn Elizabeth (Leach) Buffie; married James Macfarlane (a teacher), August 9, 1968; children: Christine Anne. *Education:* University of Manitoba, received degree, 1967, certificate in education, 1976.

ADDRESSES: Home and office—165 Grandview St., Winnipeg, Manitoba, Canada R2G 0L4.

CAREER: Hudson's Bay Co., Winnipeg, Manitoba, Canada, illustrator, 1968-70; Winnipeg Art Gallery, Winnipeg, painting instructor, 1974-75; River East School Division, Winnipeg, high school art teacher, 1976-77; freelance illustrator and painter, 1977-84; writer, 1984—.

MEMBER: Writers' Union of Canada, Canadian Authors Association, Canadian Society of Children's Authors, Illustrators, and Performers.

AWARDS, HONORS: Young Adult Canadian Book Award, 1987-88; Ontario Arts Council grants, 1987 and 1989. Works placed on Notable Canadian Young

limited in one way or another: regional areas (*Who's Who in the East*) for instance; professions (*Who's Who in Finance and Industry*); or special categories (*Who's Who of American Women*). Marquis also publishes historical volumes as companions to *Who's Who in America.* These volumes, entitled *Who Was Who in America,* began coverage (of notable Americans) with the year 1607.

Authors

There are several sources of biographical information that deal specifically with authors. The Gale Research Company publishes the *Author Biographies Master Index*, which is similar to the *Biography and Genealogy Master Index* discussed above. Another useful Gale publication is *Contemporary Authors* (Figure 12.5), which includes authors of nontechnical works, living or deceased. As of volume 160, 1998, the set includes more than 100,000 authors. A cumulative index for volumes 1 to 160 is available as a separate volume. Other author biographical dictionaries are *European Authors, 1000-1900*, edited by Stanley J. Kunitz and Vineta Colby; *Twentieth Century Authors* (with supplements), edited by Stanley J. Kuntz and Howard Haycraft; and *World Authors, 1950–70* (supplement to previous title), edited by John Wakeman.

Additional Information

There are more specific biographical dictionaries published. Some include only living persons, some only deceased, some are combined lists, some are by profession and some by country or geographical region. Some examples include: *American Men and Women of Science, Dictionary of American Biography, Current Biography* (Figure 12.6), and *Who's Who in the Socialist Countries of Europe*. For more information about biographical dictionaries in the library consult one or more of the guides to references sources discussed earlier. *Guide to Reference Books*, edited by Balay, includes many biographical dictionaries with descriptions (see its section AH pp. 281–317, 11th edition).

Other sources of biographical information in all libraries have been discussed in previous chapters. Encyclopedias, both general and subject (see Chapter 7), have biographies. Biographical information, including obituaries, is available in newspapers. Consult the index to the newspaper. Look under "Deaths" to find obituaries. The *New York Times* has published a volume indexing all obituaries that appeared from 1858 to 1968, a supplement for 1969 to 1978 and supplements to 1996. The *Personal Name Index to the New York Times* is the best source for finding personal names (and thus biographical information) that appeared in the *New York Times*. The main set includes all names that appeared until 1974. A supplement brings the set up to 1989. The *New York Times* does

Figure 12.6 Current Biography

TERESA, MOTHER Aug. 27, 1910–Sept. 5, 1997 Roman Catholic nun known as "the saint of Calcutta"; born of Albanian parents in Yugoslavia; while teaching at a convent school in Calcutta, India, in the 1940s, began rescuing abandoned and destitute terminally ill people from the gutters of the city's slums, so that they might die in peace and with dignity; attracted volunteer helpers, whom she organized in 1950 into the Missionaries of Charity, dedicated to an austere life of "wholehearted free service to [and among] the poorest of the poor—to Christ in his distressing disguise"; over the following decades, expanded her work in India and internationally to an estimated 500 orphanages, hospices for the poor (including unwed pregnant young women), the crippled, and the ill and dying (including AIDS patients and lepers), and other charity centers—not counting numerous mobile clinics—operating in approximately 100 countries by more than 4,000 nuns, 400 priests and brothers, and hundreds of lay volunteers; was awarded the Nobel Peace Prize in 1979; died in Calcutta, where she was given a state funeral in a sports stadium, attended by some 12,000 (including world dignitaries) and viewed on television by millions worldwide. See *Current Biography* (September) 1973.

Obituary *New York Times* p1+ Sept. 6, 1997

not publish or approve of the *Personal Name Index*. Another useful source of biographical information is the *Essay and General Literature Index* (see Chapter 9). Also many periodicals include biographical information. To locate biographical articles, use the periodical indexes (see Chapter 8). Biographies also may be located by using bibliographies (see Chapter 5).

Internet Sources

Some of the print sources listed earlier in this chapter are also available on-line, either through services such as FirstSearch or through other commercial databases. For example, many items that appear in the *New York Times* are available in full text versions if you search for an individual's name on the World Wide Web. Searching for biographical information via the World Wide Web may result in finding full text information from newspapers and periodicals. Some sources such as FirstSearch or CARL must be searched through a library catalog unless you have an account with the database owner. Also try searching current biography through hwwilson.com.

Exercises for Chapter 12

1. List the biographical indexes owned by your library. Include the call numbers.
2. Using biographical indexes, biographical dictionaries and other sources owned by your library, look up the biographies of the individuals listed below. Look in at least two sources for each. Record the sources where you found the information. If the individual is not located in the first two sources, check at least three more sources. Be sure to record the name of the individual checked.
   (A) Your congressman
   (B) Your favorite author
   (C) Henry Fonda
   (D) Ed Koch
   (E) Bill Gates
3. Find the name of a pianist and then locate a biography for that person.

Important Terms in Chapter 12

obituaries

Important Books for Chapter 12

American Men and Women of Science, 18th ed. New York: R. R. Bowker, 1992–1993 (8 vols.).

Author Biographies Master Index: a consolidated index of more than 1,140,000 biographical sketches concerning authors living and dead as they appear in a selection of the principal biographical dictionaries devoted to authors, poets, journalists, and other literary figures. Ed. by Dennis La Beau. 5th ed. Detroit: Gale Research, 1997.

Biographical Dictionaries Master Index. Ed. 1, 1975–76. Detroit: Gale Research, 1975. Supplements.

Biography and Genealogy Master Index. Gale Research, 1981– . Base volumes published in 1981. Five year cumulations for 1981 to 1985, 1986 to 1990 and 1991–1995, annual volumes. Annual updates. Covers more than 250 biographical dictionaries and Who's Whos. Also available on CD.

Biography Index: A Cumulative Index to Biographical Materials in Books and Magazines. New York: H. W. Wilson, 1947– .

Contemporary Authors: A Bio-Bibliographical Guide to Current Authors and Their Works. Detroit: Gale Research, 1962– .

Current Biography. V. 1– , 1940– . New York: H. W. Wilson, 1940– (monthly except August).

Dictionary of American Biography. Published under the auspices of the American Council of Learned Societies. New York: Scribner's; London: Milford, 1928–37. 20 vols. plus index. As of 1998 there are 10 supplementary volumes plus an index to the supplements.

Dictionary of National Biography. Edited by Sir Leslie Stephen and Sir Sidney Lee. London: Smith Elder, 1908. 22 vols. Reprinted, 1938. Supplements.

Encyclopedia of World Biography. Palatine, IL: J. Heraty, 1987. Volumes 13–16 of the McGraw-Hill *Encyclopedia of World Biography*, 1973.

Kunitz, Stanley Jasspon, and Vineta Colby. *European Authors, 1000-1900: A Biographical Dictionary of European Literature*. New York: H. W. Wilson, 1967.

_____, and Howard Haycroft. *Twentieth Century Authors: A Biographical Dictionary of Modern Literature*. New York: H. W. Wilson, 1942.

Marquis Who's Who Publications, Index to Who's Who Books, 1974– . Chicago, Marquis, 1975– .

New York Times Obituary Index, 1858–1968. New York: New York Times, 1970. Supplement 1969–1978, pub. 1980. Supplement 1975–1996, pub. 1998.

Wakeman, John. *World Authors, 1950–1970; A Companion Volume to "Twentieth Century Authors."* New York: H. W. Wilson, 1975.

Who Was Who in America: A Companion Biographical Reference Work to "Who's Who in America." Chicago: Marquis. 1963– (V. 9 is 1985–1989 published in 1989). Index 1607–1989.

Who's Who in America: A Biographical Dictionary of Notable Living Men and Women. Chicago: Marquis, 1899– (biennial).

Who's Who in Finance and Industry, 1936– . Chicago: Marquis, 1936– .

Who's Who in the East: A Biographical Dictionary of Leading Men and Women in the Eastern United States. V. 1– , 1942/43. Chicago: Marquis, 1943– .

Who's Who in the Socialists Countries of Europe: A Biographical Encyclopedia of More Than 12,600 Leading Personalities in Albania, Bulgaria, Czechoslovakia, German Democratic Republic, Hungary, Poland, Romania, Yugoslavia. New York: K. G. Saur, 1989.

Who's Who of American Women: A Biographical Dictionary of Notable Living American Women. Ed. 1– , 1958–9. Chicago: Marquis, 1958– .

13. Business, Career and Consumer Information

Objectives

After studying this chapter the student shall be able to
- locate firms manufacturing specific products
- locate names and addresses of companies and business organizations
- locate information about specific business, industries and organizations
- use consumer-advocate publications to find information about products
- locate information about careers and occupations

General Information

This chapter deals with the location of information about manufacturers, retail stores, consumer-orientated organizations and other types of businesses. Finding and using this information is useful in job hunting, purchasing and consumer complaining. This chapter focuses on some specific reference books for business and consumer information. Besides the new sources introduced in this chapter, one also may wish to consult sources discussed in earlier chapters, for example the yellow pages of the telephone directory and the ads in newspapers.

Business

Thomas' Register of American Manufacturers 1997 edition with 33 volumes) has several sections. The first section (volumes 1 through 22 of the 1997 edition) is a list of products and services available from the various companies by type of company. For example, if the names of knitting mills in an area are needed, one should look in *Thomas' Register* under "knit goods," where there is a listing by states of the names and addresses of knitting mills. The next section, company profiles (volumes 23 and 24), is an alphabetical listing of companies including addresses and phone numbers. The third, and last, section (volumes 25 to 33, the "Thom Cat") contains the catalogs of about 10 percent of the included companies. If one desires a new valve for a water heater and there is no local distributor for that manufacturer, the catalog contains the address and phone number of the manufacturer. Many manufacturers' catalogs include diagrams, pictures and part numbers. The *Register* also may be useful in providing the names, addresses and phone numbers of firms involved in a specific type of business. This kind of listing is helpful to individuals looking for a job in a specific industry.

Dun & Bradstreet, an agency supplying credit information and credit ratings, publishes several useful directories. For example, their *Million Dollar Directory* lists corporations with a net worth of $1,000,000 or more. The directory lists businesses alphabetically and gives the following information for each business: the address, the phone number, the number of employees, the annual sales, the type of business and names (with titles) of the executives. There are a variety of indexes enabling the user to identify businesses by type, geographical area and executives' names. These indexes make it easy to locate firms of certain types in specific geographical areas; for example, all the photographic suppliers in New England.

Dun & Bradstreet also publishes the *Middle Market Directory,* which includes businesses whose net worth is $500,000 to $999,999. This directory lists information like *the Million Dollar Directory.*

The Moody's manuals, covering a dozen topics such as public utilities, transportation and banks and finance, give lengthy reports about the businesses included. The articles include a corporate history, information on stocks, financial status and statements, management and other information. Moody's manuals are published by Dun & Bradstreet.

The Standard & Poor's Register of Corporations, Directors and Executives is a directory to American and Canadian businesses and generally

Thomas' Register **is often found on its own carrell for ease of use.**

gives the same type of information found in the Dun & Bradstreet directories.

David Brownstone's *Where to Find Business Information* is an international listing of English language publications dealing with business and industry. It includes sources such as newsletters, trade and general periodicals, books and computerized databases. This volume is an annotated bibliography with indexes leading the user to those sources (books, newsletters and periodicals) that should provide answers to specific questions.

Organizations-Profit, Nonprofit, etc.

The Encyclopedia of Associations issues a new edition approximately every other year. Volume 1 (which has several physical volumes) is the *National Organizations of the United States.* It is arranged by subject (a classified list) and includes a keyword index to the organization's name. Volume 2 is *Geographic and Executive Indexes. The* geographic index section lists all organizations in volume 1 alphabetically by state and city. The executive index is a list of executives listed in volume one, arranged

Resources on careers and colleges may be in a special section. Some of these resources may circulate.

alphabetically by surnames. Volume 3 is *New Associations and Projects* and is a supplement to volume 1. Volume 4 is *International Organizations*. There is a seven volume guide to regional, state and local organizations. Entries in volumes 1, 3 and 4 provide the full name of the association, the address and phone number, the name of the director and a description of the association. The description may include the following types of information: date founded, number of members, number of staff, publications, committees, annual meetings and conventions, and a brief history of the organization. The keyword index enables the user to identify the organization even if only one word of the organization's name is known. The classified format provides a means of locating all organizations of a similar type without knowing the names of any specific organizations.

Career Information

Most libraries have at least a few sources of information about careers. Most public libraries will have a special section with career information. Some of these sources circulate but in general they are for library use only. The U.S. Department of Labor Statistics, *Occupational Outlook Handbook* provides descriptions of occupations, professional and non-professional. Descriptions include nature of the work; working conditions; employment; training, other qualifications and advancement; job outlook; earnings; related occupations; and sources of additional information. Career sections may also include information on internships, directories of job hotlines, and handbooks with practice civil service or military tests. For examples of specific titles, see the list at the end of this chapter. For career information on the internet try the following sites: www.ajb.dni.us/ and www.occ.com.

Consumer Information

Government agencies at several levels publish information guides. Some publications deal with specific products or industries, while others are directories of sources of information. Some useful directories and other reports are published by groups not associated with any government, such as groups coordinated by Ralph Nader. For examples of specific books see the bibliography at the end of this chapter.

There are also several journals devoted to the consumer. The most widely known is *Consumer Reports,* a monthly magazine reporting on all sorts of products. This magazine lacks association with any company or governmental agency and contains tests and reports on consumer products. *Consumer Reports* also publishes an annual buyer's guide. Independent publications of this type provide useful, unbiased information on consumer goods. Smart consumers research before making major purchases such as a car, television or major appliance. Wise consumers also know that they can complain and that they have rights when products are defective. Using reference sources such as those discussed or listed in the bibliography helps the consumer in locating information when it is needed, e.g., names, addresses and phone numbers of corporations, governmental agencies or private groups that can answer questions or provide assistance. In researching business or consumer information, periodicals and newspapers (Chapter 8) and government documents (Chapter 11) also provide information. The indexes to periodicals *(Business Periodicals Index),* the *Monthly Catalog* (for federal documents, especially the Consumer Protection Agency, see Chapter 11) and newspaper indexes (e.g., those of the *New York Times* and the *Wall Street Journal)* are also useful sources.

Exercises for Chapter 13

1. Find the names and addresses of firms manufacturing golf clubs.
2. Locate at least one industry study and one consumer organization study on the use of air bags in automobiles.
3. Locate and record the name, address and phone number of the consumer protection group nearest to your home.
4. Locate the corporate headquarters of General Motors and the name of the chief executive.

Important Books for Chapter 13

BUSINESS

1997 American Big Business Directory. Omaha, NB: American Business Directories, 1997. 3 vols. Available in paper, magnetic tape, PC diskettes or CD-ROM. It includes over 177,000 organizations with 100 or more employees. Vol. 1 is alphabetical listing a-k, Vol. 2 is l-z, and Vol. 3 is arranged by city; S.I.C. code; alphabetical list of executives; and market planning statistics. Annual

Ammer, Christine. *Dictionary of Business and Economics*, rev. ed. New York: Free Press, 1986.

The Blackwell Encyclopedic Dictionary of Business Ethics. Cambridge, MA: Blackwell Business, 1997.

Brownstone, David M. *Where to Find Business Information: A Worldwide Guide for Everyone Who Needs the Answer to Business Questions.* 2nd ed. New York: John Wiley, 1982. Becoming dated but may still be useful.

Business Periodicals Index. New York: H. W. Wilson, 1958– , v. 1 (monthly). A cumulative subject index to periodicals in the field of accounting, advertising, banking and finance, general business insurance, labor and management, marketing and purchasing, public administration, taxation, specific businesses, industries and trades. Also available via FirstSearch or WilsonLine in some libraries.

Colin, P. H. *Dictionary of Business.* Kinderhook.i.b.d., Limited, 1995.

Consultants and Consulting Organizations Directory: A Reference Guide to More Than 24,000 Concerns and Individuals Engaged in Consultation for Business, Industry and Government, 18th ed. Detroit: Gale Research, 1998. (2 vols.)

Daniells, Lorna M., et al. *How to Find Information About Companies.* 8th ed. Washington, D.C.: Washington Researchers 1997. (3 vols)

Encyclopedia of Associations. 33rd ed. Edited by Katherine Gruber. Detroit: Gale Research, 1997.

Encyclopedia of Business Information Sources. 12th ed. Detroit: Gale Research, 1998.

Middle Market Directory, 1964– . New York: Dun & Bradstreet, Inc., 1964– .

Market House Books Staff. *A Dictionary of Business.* 2nd ed. New York: Oxford University Press, 1997.

Million Dollar Directory, 1959– . New York: Dun & Bradstreet, Inc., 1959– (annual).

The New Palgrave: A Dictionary of Economics. London: Macmillan, 1994. (4 vols.) This is the successor to the *Dictionary of Political Economy.*

Nisberg, Jay N. *Random House Handbook of Business Today.* New York: Random House, 1988.

Rosenberg, Jerry Martin. *Dictionary of Business and Management.* New York: Wiley, 1993.

Standard & Poor's Register of Corporations, Directors and Executives, United States and Canada, 1928– (annual).

Thomas' Register of American Manufacturers. New York: Thomas' Publishing, 190?– . (1997 edition has 33 volumes.)

U.S. Industrial Directory: Tile Direct Link to Industrial Products and Suppliers. New Providence, NJ: Reed International/Cahners, 1997. (3 vols.)

Wechman, Robert L. *Dictionary of Economics and Business: A Thousand Key Terms and People.* Champaign: Stipes Publishing, 1997.

World Chamber of Commerce Directory. Loveland, OH: Worldwide Chamber of Commerce Directory, 1989– (annual).

CONSUMERS

Asch, Peter. *Consumer Safety Regulations: Putting a Price on Life and Limb.* New York: Oxford University Press, 1988.

Brobeek, Stephen. *The Product Safety Book: The Ultimate Consumer Guide to Products Hazards.* Edited by Jack Gillis for the Consumer Federal of America. New York: E. P. Dutton, 1983.

Consumer Reports, May 1936– . Mt. Vernon, NY: Consumer's Union of the United States, 1936– (monthly). *Buyer's Guide* is the December issue.

Consumer's Index to Product Evaluation and Information Sources. V. 1, no. 1– , Winter 1974– (quarterly with annual cumulations).

Consumer's Resource Handbook. Washington, DC: U.S. Office of Consumer Affairs, 1997.

Directory of Government Agencies Safe-Guarding Consumer and Environment. Ed. 1, 1968– . Alexandria, VA: Scrina Press, 1968– .

Electronic Marketing and the Consumer. Edited by Robert A. Peterson. Thousand Oaks, CA: Sage Publications, 1997.

Elkington, John. *The Green Consumer: A Guide for the Environmentally Aware.* Rev. ed. New York: Penguin, 1993.

Gillis, Jack. *The Used Car Book: An Easy-to-Use-Guide to Buying a Safe, Reliable, and Economical Used Car.* Used Car Book, 1997–1998. New York: HarperPerennial, 1997.

Horvitz, Simeon L. *Legal Protection for Today's Consumer.* 2nd ed. Dubuque, IA: Kendall/Hunt, 1989.

Krohn, Lauren. *Consumer Protection and the Law: A Dictionary.* Santa Barbara, CA: ABC-Clio, 1995.

Reader's Digest Consumer Advisor: An Action Guide to Your Rights. Edited by James A. Maxwell, rev. ed. Pleasantville, NY: Reader's Digest, 1989.

Salinger, Frank M. *A Guide to State Consumer Regulation.* New York: Executive Enterprises Publications, 1989. Part of the consumer credit handbook series.

Smart Consumer's Directory. Nashville, TN: Thomas Nelson Publishers, 1994.

CAREER

American Jobs Abroad, edited by Victoria Harlow and Edward W. Knappman. Detroit: Gale Research Inc., 1994.

Barron's How to Prepare for the Civil Service Examinations. Woodbury, NY: Barron's Educational series. Exams are arranged by topic and publication dates vary.

Career Discovery Encyclopedia. Edited by Carol J. Summerfield. Chicago: J. G. Ferguson Publishing Company, 1993.

Encyclopedia of Career and Vocational Guidance. Edited by William E. Hopke. 9th ed. Chicago: J. G. Ferguson Publishing Company, 1993. (4 vols.)

Fisher, Helen S. *American Salaries and Wages Survey.* 4th ed. Detroit: Gale Research Inc., 1997.

Job Hotlines USA: The National Telephone Directory of Employer Joblines. 4th ed. Harleysville, PA: Career Communications, Inc., 1995.

Job Market Directory: National Guide to Job Information, Career Resources and Labor Market Data. Harleysville, PA: Career Communications, Inc., 1994.

Krantz, Les. *The World Almanac Job Finder's Guide,* 1997, World Almanac Books. New York: St. Martin's Press, 1996.

Occupational Outlook Handbook. U. S. Department of Labor, 22nd ed., 1996–1997. Bureau of Labor Statistics, Washington, DC: U.S.G.P.O. 1947– . (Biennial).

Peterson's Internships, 1998: More than 40,000 Opportunities to Get an Edge in Today's Competitive Job Market. 18th ed. Princeton, NY: Peterson's, 1997.

14. Nonprint Materials and Special Services

Objectives

After studying this chapter the student shall be able to
- recognize the formats of microfilm and microfiche and explain how they may be used
- use interlibrary loans to access remote materials
- use the OCLC system to locate materials
- request computer searches when needed

Nonprint Materials

Most libraries lump many things under the term *nonprint*. Often the term includes everything that is not a book or a periodical (that is, not printed on paper). The term then includes a variety of microprint formats; also records, audiotapes, videotapes, films and slides. Some libraries even lend the equipment needed for using these nonprint materials, such as microprint readers and cassette players.

The materials in microprint (reduced size) come in several formats. Microfilm is 16mm or 35mm and on reels. Microfiche is usually a 4 × 6 transparent card. The size of print on both microfilm and microform is usually reduced 24 times. Some microfiche is reduced 48 times. Ultrafiche is similar to microfiche, but the size of the card may be 3 × 5 or 4 × 6 and the print is reduced 98 times. An ultrafiche (3 × 5) can

169

Microfiche are found in cabinet drawers, usually near the microform readers.

contain up to 1,000 pages. Microcards can be 3×5, 4×6 or 5×8 in size but are opaque rather than transparent and may have printing on both sides of the card. Mechanical readers are needed to use all microforms. Some readers can be used with more than one format. Others are printers. They can be used to make "hard" or paper copy from the microform. The type of microform (negative or positive) and the type of copier will decide the format of the hard copy. Most microforms are positive, black letters on a white background. Some copiers use a dry photographic process so that the hard copy will be the opposite of what is seen on the screen. Positive film produces a negative image (white letters on a black background) hard copy. Some companies have designed reader/printers that are similar to photocopying machines and the hard copy is identical with what is seen on the screen. One brand of machine also senses if the microform is negative or positive and always produces a positive hard copy. These machines use plain paper which produces more permanent and readable copy.

Most readers have pictures or diagrams showing how to use the reader. If the directions are unclear or any doubt exists about the operation of the equipment, the user should request assistance from a member of the library staff. Improper use of equipment or the use of the wrong equipment can result in damage to the microform or the reader.

Special Library Services

Libraries provide services besides housing information. They provide reserve, reference and interlibrary loans. Reserves may range from holding a book that has been out in circulation to setting aside many books for a class. Reference services help users find the answers to questions. The help may vary from using the card catalog or OPAC to doing computer searches of databases. Most such searches available are of databases used to produce periodical indexes. These searches are generally faster and more complete than manual searches. Most libraries charge a fee for this type of service. One database in widespread use is PsycLIT (on-line and CD-ROM versions of *Psychological Abstracts*). From it one can obtain a computer generated list of summaries of all the journal articles on a particular topic. To obtain this information the searcher must provide key terms — descriptors — that are entered into the computer. The method is progressive in that the topic must be narrowed until the precise information can be processed. Usually librarians will

Microfilm/microfiche readers are easy to use. Some readers are also printers.

All kinds of music CDs are available in public libraries.

provide professional help to do these searches, since it requires some experience to handle the terminal and to choose and enter appropriate descriptors. Some libraries have computer terminals available for student use. For more information, see chapters 9 and 15 on CD-ROM, databases and computers in libraries.

Interlibrary loan (ILL) is a procedure for borrowing books, periodicals and other materials from other libraries. It is extremely helpful in obtaining information not available locally. Each library has its own rules for interlibrary loans and it is probably necessary to ask at the reference or interlibrary loan librarian's desk for the forms and procedures to use. Some libraries charge for interlibrary loan service and others do not.

To speed up the processing of requests for ILL the student or faculty member should provide complete information. If for example, a book is being requested, provide the author's complete name, the title of the book, publisher and date of publication. A request for a book by Jones, no first name or initial, even if the title, publisher and date are provided probably will be returned to the requester with a statement that there is insufficient information to process the request. If the needed material is a journal article, the requester must provide complete information: the full title of the journal with the volume number, date and pages, and the author's name and the title of the article. If the information is incomplete, the librarian is likely to return the request for additional information. Many librarians ask for a *verification*. The verification denotes where the user found the citation. Some libraries will not even begin to process on ILL request if the verification is not supplied. A valid verification would be any type of reference source discussed in this book.

If the request is for a book, the book will be sent. But, if the request is for a journal article, a photocopy will be sent. The time from presentation of the request to the ILL desk until the material arrives will be determined by the system(s) used by the borrowing library. For regional loans, local delivery systems are frequently used and the elapsed time probably will be short. If the requested materials must come from a distant library, the lending library will be shipping the materials either by the U.S. Postal Service or United Parcel Service. Library materials shipped in either of these ways usually takes longer to arrive at the borrowing library. For fast service, some libraries will fax a copy of journal articles. This service frequently carries a charge. Students should plan ahead.

OCLC

OCLC, is an international on-line database of the holdings of more than 32,900 libraries in 63 countries. The OCLC headquarters and computers are located in Dublin, Ohio. The member libraries include the Library of Congress, the National Library of Medicine, the National Library of Canada and the British Lending Library. They provide cataloging information that is available then to all members. The system has more than 40 million records of all types of library materials: books, periodicals, pamphlets, records, audio tapes, videotapes, government documents, etc. OCLC numbers are assigned as new items are cataloged. The OCLC database may be searched in many ways: by author's name, title, author-title, series title, OCLC number, SuDoc number, ISBN number, ISSN number, LC card number and CODEN. ISBN is the international standard book number, and ISSN is the international standard serial number. CODEN is a code assigned to serials by indexing services such as *Biological Abstracts* and *Chemical Abstracts*.

The OCLC system provides member libraries with catalog cards and or magnetic tape of their holdings for use in the member library. Each record in the OCLC database has a holding's list attached to it.

Public libraries have large and varied collections of videotapes.

Thus every member library that has a copy of *War and Peace* will have its symbol attached to the record. If a library does not own a copy of *War and Peace* it can call up the record and see which libraries own a copy. Each edition, translation, etc., of *War and Peace* will have its own record and holding's list. Besides cataloging information and printing cards, the system simplifies transmitting interlibrary loan requests between member libraries. It also checks in periodicals, produces union lists of serials by regions or other specific areas and searches other databases from which periodical indexes are produced. One of OCLC's most popular services is FirstSearch. It is available in more than 14,450 libraries in 50 countries and in early 1999 had 75 different databases available. WorldCat is the database most frequently searched. It is OCLC's main database with more than 40 million records. Other databases and services available via FirstSearch include: the most recent 90 days of articles from the *New York Times* and abstracts since 1994; NetFirst, a subject access to Internet resources; full text sources which include more than one million newspaper and journal articles for immediate viewing or e-mail delivery; electronic reference files which include encyclopedias, almanacs, directories and phone books. The subscribing libraries can subscribe to a few or all of the databases available on FirstSearch. Pricing options also allow individuals to search FirstSearch by subscription or by per-search. The holdings symbols for all libraries holding the item (book or periodical) are included in the display of each citation. Many databases available via OCLC are also accessible from DIALOG and other vendors. A library or individual can buy searches for FirstSearch at a fixed rate per search, there are no connect times or per item charges. OCLC charges for all services provided. Members of OCLC may participate in different components of the program.

Exercises for Chapter 14

1. Make a note of the ILL procedures and regulations in your library. Be sure to check on charges and the average length of time before requested materials arrive.
2. Ask the reference librarian if your library is a member of OCLC. If yes, ask about the scope of your library's participation in OCLC services.

Important Terms in Chapter 14

database	*nonprint*
OCLC	*microfiche*
interlibrary loan (ILL)	*microfilm*
ultrafiche	*verification*
microcards	*readers*

Important Books for Chapter 14

Boucher, Virginia. *Interlibrary Loan Practices Handbook*. 2nd ed. Chicago: American Library Association, 1997.

Burwell, Helen P., and Carolyn N. Hills. *Directory of Fee-Based Information Services*. Houston, TX: Burwell Enterprises, 1984– (annual).

Guide to Microforms in Print. Westport, CT: Meckler, 1961– (annual). Author-title vol., subject volume and supplements.

Internet-Plus Directory of Express Library Services: Research and Document Delivery for Hire. Chicago: American Library Association, 1997.

Jackson, Mary E., ed. *Research Access Through New Technology*. New York: AMS Press, 1989.

Morris, Leslie R., and Sandra Chass Morris. *Interlibrary Loan Policies Directory*. 5th ed. New York: Neal-Schuman Publishers, 1995. Each entry lists policies, charges, address, phone numbers, FAX numbers, etc. for over 2,000 libraries. Directory is arranged by states.

Olle, James G. *A Guide to Sources of Information in Libraries*. Brookfield, VT: Gower Publishing, 1984.

Thompson, Sarah Katherine. *Interlibrary Loan Procedure Manual*. Chicago: Interlibrary Loan Committee, American Library Association, 1975.

15. On-Line Computer Use in Libraries and Schools

Objectives

After studying this chapter the student shall be able to
- identify where computers are used in the library
- identify available computer services in the library
- locate books and journals on computers
- recognize how databases are used

Definitions

Below are listed several terms commonly used in the discussion of computers.

Password— a secret word or symbol to be typed into a computer that allows the operator access to the system and prevents unauthorized access.

Program— instructions to the computer enabling the computer to perform desired tasks.

Hardware— the physical equipment: the computer, monitor, keyboard, etc.

Software— programs for the computer.

Keyboard— device for entering information into a computer by depressing keys. Computer keyboards are similar to typewriter keyboards.

Monitor— a screen for observing, viewing or controlling the operation of the computer. Most look very much like a TV screen. They may be colored or monochromatic (one color, usually green or amber).

Printer— a device that prints information from the computer; used to produce a "hard" (paper) copy of the desired data.

Floppy Disk (Diskette)— a flat circular plate with a magnetic surface, usually enclosed in a square paper envelope or plastic case. Data (information) may be stored on one or both sides.

Modem— a device used to transmit computer signals over communication (usually telephone) facilities.

Peripherals— any device outside the central processing unit (disk drives, printers, monitors, etc.).

General Information

Most libraries use computers for a variety of tasks. A few libraries restrict computers use to staff only but most libraries have many computers available for public use. Those libraries having computers for public use provide a wide range of assistance, including general instruction, formal classes and instruction sheets at each terminal. The kind and number of computer resources available and regulations regarding use vary from library to library. Many school libraries use Apple computers and most public libraries use PCs.

Regulations on the use of computers differ, as do the types of software owned by the library. Most public libraries do not allow sign-up for computer searching (usually Internet or e-mail) for more than a week in advance and usually limit access to less than one hour. These services are very popular and resources are limited.

Some libraries might require a user to indicate their familiarity with computers or the Internet before they are allowed access. Instruction in formal classes or a short orientation session with the equipment may be required. This permits most users to become familiar with the operation of the equipment. These restrictions may apply to all users.

Database searching is available in many libraries. It might be from CD-ROMs on site or via the Internet. It might also include some of the commercial vendors such as DIALOG (which charge by the minute). Using the Internet to access some services such as OCLC's FirstSearch or DIALOG usually eliminates the cost of a long distance phone call. For more information about the Internet and FirstSearch refer back to parts of chapters 2, 3, 8, 9, 11, 12 and 14. If a commercial source such as DIALOG is searched, generally the librarian does the searching since the system is complex and costly if the search is not properly formulated. Searches from commercial vendors can be printed while on-line or printed off-line and mailed to the library. The off-line printing tends to be much less expensive and the few days delay in viewing the results is acceptable to most users. In school media centers there is often a charge for printing results from an on-line search or a search of a CD-ROM on site. Many public libraries and some college and university libraries also charge for printing. The reasons vary but generally include discouraging the printing of non-required information, the cost of paper and cartridges for the printer. With proper equipment and a willingness to pay the bill, searching can be done from home.

The catalog should be consulted for books on computers. For libraries using the Library of Congress system, most books will be in the QA76s; in Dewey libraries, books will be in the 000s and the 510s. These are not the only locations, so the catalog should be checked. Libraries may have journals on computers and computing. The periodicals list contains the items the library subscribes to that deal with computers. Other popular computer magazines include: *Computer World; Byte; Personal Computing; Home Office Computing; InfoWorld; PC World; Internet World; PC Magazine; Smart Computing; Windows95 Magazine; Macworld; Family PC; and Computer Shopper.*

Exercises for Chapter 15

1. Determine if your library has computers. If so, what kind?
2. Who is allowed to use the equipment?
3. List the rules for software use in your library.
4. List the rules for using the computers in your library.
5. To what computer periodicals does your library subscribe?
6. If your school doesn't have any computers in the library, check the public library and see what it has.

Important Terms in Chapter 15

database	*hardware*
software	*microcomputer*
vendor	*peripherals*
terminal	*printer*
monitor	*floppy disk (diskette)*
modem	*keyboard*
password	

Important Books for Chapter 15

Alberico, Ralph. *Microcomputers for the Online Searcher: Media and Tools for Value-Added Online Searching Small Computers in Libraries.* Westport, Ct.: Meckler Corp., 1987.

Barrett, Daniel J. *Net Research: Finding Information Online.* Sebastopol, CA: Songline Studies: O'Reilly and Associates, 1997.

Books and Periodicals Online: A Directory of Online Publications. 2 volumes. Washington, DC: Library Technology Alliance, 1997.

Connors, Martin. *Online Database Search Services Directory*, 2nd edition. Detroit: Gale Research, 1988.

Daniel, Evelyn H. *Media and Microcomputers in the Library: A Selected Annotated Resource Guide.* Phoenix, AZ: Oryx, 1984.

Directory of Online Databases. Santa Monica, CA: Cuadra Associates, 1979- . Volume 1- , Fall 1979- .

Downing, Douglas A.; Michael A. Covington and Melody Mauldin Covington. *Dictionary of Computer and Internet terms.* 5th edition. Barron's Educational Series, Inc. Hauppauge, NY: 1996.

Gilster, Paul. *Digital Literacy.* New York: Wiley Computer Pub., 1997.

_____. *Finding It on the Internet: The Internet Navigator's Guide to Search Tools and Techniques.* Rev. and expanded, 2nd ed. New York: Wiley Computer Pub., 1996.

Hahn, Harley. *Harley Hahn's the Internet Complete Reference.* 2nd ed. Berkeley: Osborne McGrawHill, 1996.

_____. *The Internet Yellow Pages.* 3rd ed. Berkeley: Osborne McGrawHill, 1996.

Internet Culture. Edited by David Porter. New York: Routledge, 1997.

Kesselman, Martin and Sarah Watstein. *End-User Searching: Services and Providers.* Chicago: American Library Association, 1988.

Krol, Ed. *The Whole Internet User's Guide and Catalog.* Adapted by Bruce C. Klopfenstein. Belmont, CA: Integra Media Group; Sebastopol, CA: O'Reilly, 1996.

Software Review, v. 1- . Westport, CT: Meckler, 1982- .

Thacker, Kathleen, ed. *Directory of Computerized Data Files.* Springfield, VA: National Technical Information, U.S. Department of Commerce, 1989.

16. Hints for Writing Papers

Objectives

After studying this chapter the student shall be able to
- use note cards as an adjunct to library research
- use a database to take notes
- label cards for retrieval and bibliography writing
- be aware of the various uses of word processors in footnoting, outlining, indexing and composing papers
- find an appropriate method for citing other authors
- distinguish between primary and secondary sources and know the advantage of using primary sources
- define and avoid plagiarism
- understand copyright and the rules governing the photocopying of material

General Information

Writing term papers and reports can be a laborious process, particularly is the writer does not use efficient methods of data collection and retrieval. Thus, it is important to develop techniques that will enable one to avoid unnecessary work. The following discussion is not meant as a comprehensive discourse on how to write term papers since there are many excellent term paper manuals that may be consulted for this purpose. Rather, hints that the authors have found useful in writing papers are presented.

Taking Notes with Note Cards

The first step to writing the paper is to conceptualize the topic. Research in the library follows. How to find materials has been discussed extensively in the prior chapters. Gathering and transcribing data in a useful form so that it may be retrieved later must be done efficiently. One extremely useful way of saving data is by using lined index cards. Each piece of data should be abstracted and transcribed to cards, preferably the 4 x 6 or the 5 x 8 cards. This may sound simple minded and one may ask why notebook paper is not equally good. Using cards has several advantages. First, a card or set of cards can be easily sorted by topics later and then resorted using other categories; this is more difficult with notebook paper. Second, more materials on the same topic or from the same source may be added more easily later by just adding cards. Third, when writing an outline cards may be sorted by subheadings.

For writing note cards, the following hints will be helpful. Include on the first card for each source the information that will be needed in the footnote and the bibliography. On each subsequent card for the source show the author and the date of the work at the top. This will save all the accumulated work that has already been done in case the cards get dropped or mixed up. Frequently when doing research reviews, one may find several articles by the same author written at different times. When the paper is written it is difficult to recall from which articles that piece of information derives, thus the need for the author and date on each card.

Taking Notes with a Database

Using a database for note taking can be an invaluable aid to the student. Databases allow information to be stored in records and fields. Each record contains all the information about a particular source, magazine article, book or reference citation. Within each record, many fields may be designated to contain selected information about that record. Thus, for each source, there is a record with multiple fields.

As the student finds additional articles, he can enter the information about the article into the database by record. A typical record might look like the following:

Record #1

Field Name

Author	Mills, Frederick A.
Title	"Databasing for Fun and Profit"
Journal	*Popular Databasing*
Date	July 1985
Volume #	7:12
Pages	35–43
Content	This article contains information about the newest databases available; with emphasis on their application at home.
Subject	Databases

Other fields may be added as needed. The better databases allow 20 or more fields for each record. Once the information has been entered (this can be done a little at a time) it can be selected in a variety of ways for later use by sorting by any of the fields. Sorting the above record by author will give the bibliographic references necessary for the report.

Another sort by subject provides clusters of records that form sections of chapters to be written. Another sorting by date would be helpful in writing in a time or historic framework. Instead of carrying around many individual index cards, the student can store all the information necessary for writing the paper on a single diskette.

The fields and records may be output to a printer in any way the user desires. For example, a printed list with just the authors' names, or just the names of the journal articles, could be printed out. Furthermore, the format is flexible so that the spacing and line setups can be determined by the author. As more entries are added to the database the information is automatically added, and revised copies of the lists can be printed out in a matter of minutes. This feature alone could save hours of sorting and typing.

The writer must learn to use the database. But this time is well spent. No special knowledge of the computer is necessary to begin working with a database. Anyone can sit at the computer, follow the instruction manual and begin databasing in a matter of minutes. More involved use of the program will become evident as the student uses a program more. Usually, students may obtain databases from school or purchase them at minimal cost.

Word Processing

Students should use word processors to construct papers and theses. These are readily available for loan or may be purchased inexpensively. Writing a paper using a word processor takes most of the drudgery out of the process. It allows for instant corrections as you are typing. This takes the fear out of the process and greatly increases one's typing speed and confidence at the keyboard. Editing can be done directly on the keyboard or from a hard (printed) copy of the text. Words can be changed, sentences moved, paragraphs may be added or deleted instantaneously and the revised version can be printed out immediately. Large amounts of text can be stored on floppy disks rather than on reams of paper and large numbers of index cards. Many word processing packages provide a spelling checker integrated into the software package which will automatically check the spelling of all words in the text. Some programs even offer substitute words to use. Most word processors also include a thesaurus that provides synonyms. One merely points to a word in the text, hits a key and a list of substitutes appear.

Also one may use a word processor for other purposes besides composing documents. Footnoting is easy using a word processing program such as WordPerfect or Word. The program allows footnotes to cross-reference documents in many ways. The reader can be informed to seek additional information on other pages, in other chapters, in other paragraphs and in end notes. An automatic reference numbering system allows the writer to renumber his footnotes automatically as new ones are added or deleted.

As one is writing, key words or phrases may be marked for later use in a table of contents or for indexes at the back of the book. WordPerfect has a feature for outlining that automatically creates the necessary levels using Roman numerals, letters and many subdivisions. Paragraphs may be numbered for future editing, graphics may be inserted into text and calculations may be done without leaving the program. As with the databases, some time must be spent learning to use a word processor, but again the time will be well spent. The reason for this will become apparent when one writes just one paper on the word processor.

Libraries host a variety of activities as illustrated by these Scrabble players.

Footnoting

Deciding what must be footnoted or cited is a difficult decision. Authors are entitled to credit for their work, just as the student wants a grade or credit for the paper he or she has written. It is unfair, immoral and may be illegal to use information written by another author without giving the appropriate credit to the author. Some information is common knowledge and does not have to be cited. For example, the name of the 13th president of the United States, dates of important events and other data are so widely known that authors need not give credit. This kind of information, though one has to look it up, need not be cited. Still, specific information, such as an author's written opinion and other unique productions such as research findings should always be cited. On should never copy from another work unless it is made clear that the material is a quotation and the author is cited.

When reusing information from another source, it is still necessary to cite the author even if the words that are used by the student are different. If the idea was found in someone else's work, it must be cited. It is not only ethically and morally an imperative, but copying without citation could result in dire consequences to the student. All colleges

Using the copy machine.

have several rules against copying or, as it is called, plagiarism. Students have been expelled or given a failing grade because their papers had been known to contain material that was plagiarized. A college handbook is a good source of information on the college's policy on plagiarism.

Copying from a source without credit is analogous to stealing. But one can avoid the problem. Whenever there is the slightest doubt as to whether one should cite something, cite it. It is preferable to cite too much than to omit a citation that is necessary.

One simple and widely used method of notation consists of inserting parenthetically the author's last name, a comma and the date directly in the text as needed. For example, a study has shown that boys and girls do not significantly differ in total reading ability at the 8th grade level (Wolf, 1978).

This seems a logical way to cite works by other authors. However, instructors may insist on a particular format for citations and bibliographic listings, and the student should make sure that they use the required format. If the instructor lacks preference, the student could well use the method described above for citations and the bibliographic style that is found after each chapter in this text. Anyhow, one must get the information correctly transcribed the first time, since it may be extremely difficult to find it later. Transcribe the bibliographic information plus the citation onto the first card exactly as it should appear in the final paper. This will make it easier when the paper is written. Use as many cards as necessary for that source, putting the citation on each card. For example, "(World, 1975)." A numbering system also will be useful with multiple cards.

Primary Sources

To develop precision in researching a topic the student should use as many primary resources as possible. Primary sources are those that are written or reported by the author. Secondary sources, on the other hand, are reports, abstracts or descriptions based on the primary sources or taken from the primary source. Primary sources may often be more accurate than secondary sources, particularly where the secondary source extensively summarizes the original material. Secondary source writers may misquote, misinterpret or distort the original materials. This usually occurs in reviews of the literature in a particular field. For example, in the *Annual Review of Psychology* the reviewer must abstract one dozen research articles on a topic such as psychotherapy. Often in condensing the findings, gross errors occur as well as subtle differences in meaning.

Researchers should find out whether the information being obtained derives from a primary or secondary source. Detective work should reveal original sources that provide more accurate data. These should be consulted when possible.

Copyright

Copyright is a means of protecting the rights of authors, composers and artists. Copyright laws protect original works from being copied, except for specific conditions outlined in the law, and insure that the individual creating the copyrighted materials receives payment (royalties) for the sale of his or her works. The copyright law is specific in detailing requirements for receiving a copyright (the copyright office is a part of the Library of Congress), and in the placement of the copyright statement in published materials. To locate copyright information in published materials, look on the title page or the back of the title page for the date. The law is also specific about the conditions for reproducing copyrighted materials and the penalty for violating the law. The law provides for stiff penalties for infringement on the rights of the copyright owners (author or publisher) when copies are made without the written permission of the copyright owner. Today's high quality, rapid photocopying machines provide the means of violating the law, and students and faculty should not make multiple copies of protected materials without permission. A single copy of a page or two of a journal article or a book, to be used for scholarly purposes, is usually permissible. Yet, credit should be given to the author and permission obtained from the copyright owner. This may be obtained by writing the publisher. Under no conditions should multiple copies be made without the permission of the publisher.

Term Paper Guides (see also Chapter 5)

Bolner, Myrtle S. *The Research Process: Books and Beyond*. Rev. print. Dubuque, Iowa: Kenall/Hunt Pub. Co., 1997.

Fleischer, Eugene R. *A Style Manual for Citing Microform and Nonprint Media*. Chicago: American Library Association, 1978.

Lunsford, Andrea, and Robert Connors. *The St. Martin's Handbook*. 3rd ed. New York: St. Martin's Press. 1996. (This volume contains several style sheets including the American Psychological Association and the Modern Language Association.)

MLA Handbook for Writers of Research Papers, 4th ed. Edited by Joseph Gibaldi and Walter S. Achtert. New York: Modern Language Association, 1997.

Slade, Carole. *Form and Style: Theses, Reports, Term Papers*, 10th ed. Houghton, 1997.

Taylor, Gordon. *The Student's Writing Guide for the Arts and Social Sciences*. New York: Cambridge University Press, 1989.

Turabian, Kate L. *A Manual for Writers of Term Papers, Theses, and Dissertations*, 6th ed. Chicago: University of Chicago Press, 1996.

Appendix: Answers to Exercises

Chapter 1

Each library will differ in layout and regulations

Chapter 2

1. Golf (LCSH 1996 v. 2 p. 2200)
   (May subd geog) GV961–GV987
   BT   Ball Games
   SA subdivisions Golf *under names of individual educational institutions*
   e.g.
   NT   Caddies
        Caddying
        Golfers
        .
        .

        .
        Wedge Shot
   —   Accidents and injuries
        —   USE Golf injuries
   —   Betting (May subd geog)
        —   BT Sports Betting
   —   Coaching (May subd geog)
        UF   Golf coaching
        BT   Coaching (Athletics)

— Drive [GV979.D74]
   UF Drive (Golf)
       Driving (Golf)

     .

     .

     .

— Training (May subd geog)
   BT Physical education and training

2. (A) Q 121 M3
   (B) PE 1625 O87
   (C) AY 67 N5 W7
   (D) JK 516 C57
   (E) AG 5 K 315

3. (A) 520
   (B) 599.9
   (C) 599.8
   (D) 000

4. (A) E-F
   (B) L
   (C) ND
   (D) NE
   (E) R
   (F) G

5. (A) 1991
   (B) Atlanta, Ga.
   (C) BM 700 N48 1991
   (D) Jacob Neusner
   (E) South Florida Studies in the History of Judaism
   (F) 2
   (G) The Enchantments of Judaism
   (H) No
   (I)   Scholars Press

Chapter 3

If you have access to an OPAC try these. The results will vary depending on the library's holdings. If your library does not have any books by Jean M. Auel, choose another author. Be sure to try question 4 even if your library has no books by Jean M. Auel. Try accessing another library via the Internet and repeat the search for books by Jean M. Auel.

Chapter 4

1. **Last Supper** (LCSH 1996 v. 3, p. 3010)
   [BT420] *Here are entered works on the final meal of Christ with his apostles...*
   UF Jesus Christ-Last Supper
   BT Dinners and dining in the Bible
   RT Lord's Supper
       Maundy Thursday
       Passover in the New Testament
   Last Supper (Mural Painting)
       USE Campos, Maria Rosatia. Santa Ceia Leonardo, da Vinci, 1452–1519. Last Supper
   Last Supper in Art
   Last Supper in literature (Not subd geog)

2. Some examples are:
   Jewish-Arab Relations (LCSH 1996 v. 2, p. 2787)
   Israel-Arab Conflicts (LCSH 1996 v. 2, p. 2731)
   Israel-Arab Border Conflicts, 1949- (LCSH 1996 v. 2, p. 2731)
   Palestinian Arabs (LCSH 1996 v. 3, p. 3948)

3. Some examples are:
   (A) Palestine-History-To 70 AD
   (B) Oil Well Drilling, Submarine (May subd geog)
   (C–E) See answers to question 1 above

4. Answers will vary depending on the topic chosen.

Chapter 5

1. (A) Poe, Edgar Allan (1,2,4 will vary from library to library) 3. Examples: Dameron, J. Lasley and Irby B. Cauthen. *Edgar Allen Poe: A Bibliography of Criticism, 1827-1967*. And Pollin, Burton R. *Dictionary of Names and Titles in Poe's collected works.*

2. (A) BIP 1997-98 v. 2, p. 4689 59 entries
   (B) CBI 1990 v. 1, p. 2106 10 entries
   (C) Political Science, Biography, Great Britain are some examples

2. Diana, Princess of Wales
   (A) BIP 1997-98 v.2, p. 3216 24 entries
   (B) Diana, Princess of Wales
        Royal Houses
        Windsor, House of

Chapter 6

1. Have you looked at this book carefully?

3. For example Morton, Andrew. *Diana: her new life*, Book Review Digest 1995 p. 1576 (2 reviews listed)

Chapter 7

Questions 1-10, 13-14 involve the varying resources of individual libraries. For 10 (C), see any of the comparative guides like those published by Barron's or Peterson.

11. (A) Yellow pages – ads, subject index. Blue pages – government agencies: local, county, state, and federal
    (B) Green pages (some green edged) – ZIP codes. Sometimes local street maps
    (C) White pages at the front (sometimes gray edged)
    (D) city street maps, airport diagrams, tourist attractions, community services, stadium and theater diagrams.

12. (B) 1992 estimate 2,832,901
    (C) 1991 census population 27,296,859, area 9,970,210 sq. km. (3,849,675 sq. mi.), 1997-98 Prime Minister Jean Chretien

Chapter 8

Questions 1–3, 7 will vary from library to library, and from student to student.

4. v. 56, 1996, p. 1111
    v. 50, p. 983
    v. 44, p. 950
    v. 39, p. 713
    v. 34, p. 563

5. 1996, v. 56, p. 1118-1119, 10 *see also* headings, 11 major subheadings, one of these has 5 subheadings. 1974-775, v. 34, p. 566, 3 *see also* headings and 3 subheadings.

6. FirstSearch (April 1998)
    Humanities Index 87 entries
    Social Sciences Index 789 entries
    Wilson Business Abstracts 1120 entries
    General Science Index 211 entries

Chapter 9

Answers will vary from library to library.

Chapter 10

1. Answers will vary from library to library. See the bibliography at the end of Chapter 10.

2. (A) For locations see *Granger's Index,* 7th ed., p. 838.
    (B) See entries in Short Story Index under Clemens, Samuel Langhorne and under Twain, Mark. Some stories are: *The Man Who*

Corrupted Hadleyburg, The California Tale, The Celebrated Jumping Frog of Calaveras County (also known as *The Notorious Jumping Frog of Calaveras County*), *The Invalid's Story, Three Thousand Years Among the Microbes, Dick Baker's Cat, Jim Baker's Bluejay Yarn*, and *Jim Blaine and His Grandfather's Ram*.

(C) Hint. Check BIP, etc. for publishing date. See *Book Review Index* 1965-84 Cumulation, v. 2, p. 973.

(D) For example see *Reader's Guide* under Motion Picture Reviews, v. 50, 1990, p. 1261.

(E) Some of the plays by Simon are: *California Suite, God's Favorite, The Good Doctor, The Odd Couple, The Prisoner of Second Avenue, The Sunshine Boys, Visitor from Forest Hills, Barefoot in the Park, Come Blow Your Horn, The Gingerbread Boy, The Last of the Red Hot Lovers, Plaza Suite, Brighton Beach Memoirs, Broadway Bound*, and *Biloxi Blues*. For reviews see: RGPL under Simon, Neil or see New York Times Index under Theater (see 1988, p. 1271 for reviews of *Biloxi Blues* and *Broadway Bound*).

(F) For example see *Essay and General Literature Index*, v. 8, p. 270–271, Clemens, Samuel Langhorne, or v. 10 under Twain, Mark, pp. 1672-1675.

Chapter 11

1. For some examples see the bibliography at the end of Chapter 11.

2. Using FirstSearch GPO file in April 1998:
   Biological Warfare 63 entries
   Whitewater investigation 28 entries

3. Check any of the following: *Congressional Directory, Congressional Staff Directory, Almanac of American Politics, Taylor's Encyclopedia*, any encyclopedia.

4. (A) Alben W. Barkley. (Examples of sources – any volume of *Taylor's Encyclopedia*, any encyclopedia)
   (B) Use the *U.S. Government Manual* or check any encyclopedia.
   (C) Check the latest volume of *Taylor's Encyclopedia*.

5. Answers will vary.

Chapter 12

1. For examples of titles see bibliography in Chapter 12.

2. (A and B) Will vary from student to student
    (C–E) Check such sources as *Biography Index, Personal Name Index to the New York Times Index, Biography and Genealogy Master Index*
    (C) see *Current Biography Cumulative Index, 1940-1995*
    (D) Bill Gates. For example see *Biography Index* v. 22, p. 152. FirstSearch (April 1998) Biography Index — Bill Gates = 70 entries and Henry Fonda = 8 entries.

2. Check the back of *Biography Index* by occupation. V. 22, p. 616-617.

Chapter 13

1. See *Thomas' Register* 1997, v. 9, pp. 17047-17050.

2. For examples see *Business Periodicals Index*, Air Bag Restraint Systems *see* Automobiles-Air Bags. 1991-1992, p. 306.

3. See a directory such as *Encyclopedia of Associations*.

4. See directories such as *Moody's Industrial Manual, Million Dollar Directory*. See index in *Moody's*, blue pages.
    General Motors
    3044 W. Grand Blvd. #10
    Detroit, Michigan 48202-3090
    Chairman, President and CEO John F. Smith
    (from *1997 American Big Business Directory* v. 1, p. 1815)

Chapters 14 and 15

Answers will vary from library to library.

Index